A Christmas Cactus

A COMEDY

by Eliot Byerrum

A SAMUEL FRENCH ACTING EDITION

FOUNDED 1830

New York Hollywood London Toronto
SAMUELFRENCH.COM

Copyright © 1991, 1995 by E. D. Byerrum

ALL RIGHTS RESERVED

CAUTION: Professionals and amateurs are hereby warned that *A CHRISTMAS CACTUS* is subject to a royalty. It is fully protected under the copyright laws of the United States of America, the British Commonwealth, including Canada, and all other countries of the Copyright Union. All rights, including professional, amateur, motion picture, recitation, lecturing, public reading, radio broadcasting, television and the rights of translation into foreign languages are strictly reserved. In its present form the play is dedicated to the reading public only.

The amateur live stage performance rights to *A CHRISTMAS CACTUS* are controlled exclusively by Samuel French, Inc., and royalty arrangements and licenses must be secured well in advance of presentation. PLEASE NOTE that amateur royalty fees are set upon application in accordance with your producing circumstances. When applying for a royalty quotation and license please give us the number of performances intended, dates of production, your seating capacity and admission fee. Royalties are payable one week before the opening performance of the play to Samuel French, Inc., at 45 W. 25th Street, New York, NY 10010.

Royalty of the required amount must be paid whether the play is presented for charity or gain and whether or not admission is charged.

Stock royalty quoted upon application to Samuel French, Inc.

For all other rights than those stipulated above, apply to: Samuel French, Inc.

Particular emphasis is laid on the question of amateur or professional readings, permission and terms for which must be secured in writing from Samuel French, Inc.

Copying from this book in whole or in part is strictly forbidden by law, and the right of performance is not transferable.

Whenever the play is produced the following notice must appear on all programs, printing and advertising for the play: "Produced by special arrangement with Samuel French, Inc."

Due authorship credit must be given on all programs, printing and advertising for the play.

ISBN 978-0-573-69517-9   Printed in U.S.A.   #5901

No one shall commit or authorize any act or omission by which the copyright of, or the right to copyright, this play may be impaired.

No one shall make any changes in this play for the purpose of production.

Publication of this play does not imply availability for performance. Both amateurs and professionals considering a production are *strongly* advised in their own interests to apply to Samuel French, Inc., for written permission before starting rehearsals, advertising, or booking a theatre.

No part of this book may be reproduced, stored in a retrieval system, or transmitted in any form, by any means, now known or yet to be invented, including mechanical, electronic, photocopying, recording, videotaping, or otherwise, without the prior written permission of the publisher.

IMPORTANT BILLING AND CREDIT REQUIREMENTS

All producers of A CHRISTMAS CACTUS *must* give credit to the Author of the Play in all programs distributed in connection with performances of the Play and in all instances in which the title of the Play appears for purposes of advertising, publicizing or otherwise exploiting the Play and/or a production. The name of the Author *must* also appear on a separate line, on which no other name appears, immediately following the title, and *must* appear in size of type not less than fifty percent the size of the title type.

A CHRISTMAS CACTUS

THE CAST

CACTUS O'RILEY:
Female private detective, redhead, quite attractive, 30s

FRED BOOKER:
Secretary to Cactus, 20s

ADELAIDE BOOKER:
Fred's mother, middle-aged

STUART WINDSOR:
Deputy District Attorney, 30s to 40s

NEVILLE SMEDLEY:
A convicted embezzler, middle-aged

RAMON RAMIREZ:
Illegal alien, very sincere, 20s

A CHRISTMAS CACTUS

TIME

The present. Late afternoon on Christmas Eve.

PLACE

Private investigator CACTUS O'RILEY's office. Shadows and lights can be seen through a window, and street sounds can be heard. A red neon sign indicates Rivers, a nearby coffeehouse. A fire escape out the window is visible to the audience. A SAXOPHONE musician offstage can be heard playing *O Little Town of Bethlehem*. A small partition divides the area between CACTUS's desk and FRED's desk. There are bookshelves, a sofa, a couple of chairs, a coat rack, a dart board and darts, and a coffee table. The office is half decorated for the holidays with some garland, and a bust of Charles Dickens - normally used as a hat stand - is festooned with a bright red ribbon. A small, green tree sits on the desk waiting for decorations. The office has a cozy, though shabby, feel to it.

AT CURTAIN

FRED is in the middle of a phone conversation with ADELAIDE. The audience hears all because they use a speaker phone. FRED has an open suitcase on his desk. HE is packing vacation brochures, swim goggles and a brightly patterned shirt with sales tags. HE goes to a bookshelf, selects a book and packs it too.

ACT 1

ADELAIDE: *(Voice-over)* Don't dawdle at the office now, dear. You know that Christmas dinner takes a lot of preparation.

FRED: It's under control, Adelaide. I'll be there.

ADELAIDE: *(Voice-over)* You haven't told me where we're going on our trip yet, Fred.

FRED: Mother! Don't you think this annual Christmas vacation thing is getting a little ... stale?

ADELAIDE: *(Voice-over)* But we do this every year. We've done it ever since your father died.

FRED: He died when I was 14!

ADELAIDE: *(Voice-over)* He never was much fun on holidays.

FRED: Wouldn't you have a better time with one of your girlfriends? And maybe then I ...

ADELAIDE: *(Voice-over)* You know how I believe in tradition, Frederick. Where are we going?

FRED: That's a surprise.

ADELAIDE: *(Voice-over)* But what should I pack? Give me a clue. *(FRED quickly closes the suitcase. HE sets it down. Meanwhile, mail is pushed through the door slot, which FRED picks up and sorts.)* Fred, I have three *lists* of things to take, one for hot weather, one for cold weather, and one for in between ...

FRED: Lists, Adelaide? You already have three different *bags* packed.

ADELAIDE: *(Voice-over)* Arizona? Vermont? Miami?
(CACTUS O'RILEY rushes into the office and hears the tail end of the conversation.) You're being so secretive this year!

FRED: I'll see you soon. Don't forget the cheeseball.
ADELAIDE: *(Voice-over)* But Fred ...
FRED: Good bye, dear.

(FRED clicks off the phone. CACTUS puts her bag down and takes off her coat.)

CACTUS: Fred, what are you doing here? It's Christmas Eve! I thought you were taking the afternoon off. I *ordered* you to take it off.

(CACTUS tosses her hat on the bust of Dickens and goes to her desk. FRED greets her with a piece of paper HE waves at her.)

FRED: I am. I have the lease renewal here. You've got to sign it and get it back. Now.
CACTUS: You've been waving it at me for a month.
FRED: Because you haven't signed it.

(SHE walks away from him, not taking it.)

CACTUS: It's not due till New Year's.
FRED: It's too late to mail. Now it's got to be hand delivered!

(Evading him, CACTUS notices the suitcase.)

CACTUS: Fred, what's this suitcase doing here?
FRED: You're changing the subject.
CACTUS: You moving in?
FRED: *(Following her, the lease still in hand.)* I don't want

Adelaide finding it accidentally. She's coming over tonight.

CACTUS: So stick it in your closet.

FRED: It's the first place she'd look! She's been pumping me for clues all week. "Where are we going? Is it hot? Is it cold?"

CACTUS: You haven't told her you've arranged separate vacations this year, have you?

FRED: I've tried, Cactus. Really I have. I've been going on a Christmas vacation with her, just the two of us, for the last *15 years.* If I don't make a break now, I'm going to be shoving off with Mother till I'm 50. I'm going to tell her tonight. It's just finding the right moment that's hard.

CACTUS: It's not going to get any easier. She'll notice you're gone.

FRED: But I got her a trip to a great spa in the Poconos. It's very nice. Really.

CACTUS: And what did my wild trailblazer here decide?

FRED: A windjammer cruise to Martinique. Warm balmy breezes, women in bikinis, no telephones, women in bikinis...

CACTUS: And Adelaide in a life preserver. I can see it now. You may find this is something she's always dreamed of ...

FRED: I'll tell her! It'll be fine, really. *(HE puts the lease on his desk, picks up the suitcase and places it out of view. HE takes up the lease again.)* How about your signature? Right here.

CACTUS: There's plenty of time.

FRED: There is not.

CACTUS: The office is now officially closed for the holidays. Adelaide will be calling.

(Playing for time, FRED rehangs a strand of tinsel on the tree.)

FRED: I just thought I'd finish the tree before I leave.

CACTUS: Oh, the tree.

FRED: *(Accusingly.)* You abandoned it. But never fear, we'll do it now.

CACTUS: Don't worry about it. It's too late.

FRED: It's never too late.

(FRED picks up an ornament from a box.)

CACTUS: Oh please! We can't all be jolly little elves ... *(SHE looks suspiciously at the bust.)* I see you've even decorated Karl Marx there. The old Communist.

FRED: It's Charles Dickens, the old Socialist! And you know it. Looks festive, doesn't he? We just got him back today.

CACTUS: So soon?

FRED: *(FRED produces another piece of paper.)* Here's the thank-you letter from St. Scolastica's for using Chuck in the library display on Dickens.

CACTUS: Too bad he wasn't here last week when the office was burglarized. They might have stolen him instead of just trashing the place.

(FRED quickly covers the ears on the statue with his hands.)

FRED: She didn't mean it, Chuck!

CACTUS: I could've filed an insurance claim for the loss of a priceless bust of Charles ... Darwin.

FRED: Dickens!

CACTUS: Wishful thinking. There is nothing worth stealing here. Why would anyone want Chuck?

FRED: You should be glad they didn't take anything.

A CHRISTMAS CACTUS

Cactus: I'm surprised they didn't leave a sympathy note. It's just like last year ... burgled under the mistletoe.
Fred: Think it's the same guys?
Cactus: Returned to the scene of the crime?

(THEY turn to each other and exchange looks.)

Fred and Cactus: Nah!
Cactus: How can you be so sure it's Dickens?

(SHE takes a closer look at the bust.)

Fred: It's one of the few things poor old Jake Marley left.
Cactus: Marley is dead, Fred.
Fred: I know that. I'm just saying Marley had a thing for Dickens. He left us the whole collection of novels here. It's Chuck, trust me. You don't like Dickens, do you? How come?
Cactus: Details, Fred. He never stops with the details! We may need to know they drink grog. We don't need to know the recipe. *(SHE reaches out to take a book and opens it, but it's dusty. SHE blows the dust off and puts it back.)* I see we're both big fans.
Fred: I am going to read one. Besides, these books are bound in leather, they're mainly for show.
Cactus: This couldn't have been opened since Marley died.
Fred: Well, dust to dust ...

(CACTUS turns away from the books and checks her purse. SHE takes her revolver out, checks the cylinder and locks it up in her desk drawer.)

CACTUS: My gun always makes this thing feel like lead.

FRED: You went shopping with Smith & Wesson? You must get great service.

CACTUS: I have got to get my shoulder holster fixed.

FRED: *(FRED picks up a stack of mail and hands her a card HE'S been saving.)* Mail call. Another Christmas card. You are so popular.

CACTUS: *(Opens the card and reads.)* "Caught in the slammer on Christmas Eve? Call your friendly bailbondsman, Steve. You'll be out in a flash, with time to repent. Merry Christmas to all, and to all 10 percent." *(SHE looks through the stack.)* Santa with a badge. Santa with a gun. Santa's a tough cookie. *(CACTUS takes a cookie. FRED has the lease again, waving it at her hopefully.) (Tentatively.)* Fred, I was thinking. What if we just closed the office?

FRED: For the holidays? Sure, things are slow right now and with me off to ...

CACTUS: No ... I mean for good.

FRED: *(Stunned.)* For good? You don't mean ... out of business?

CACTUS: That's the idea.

FRED: *(Alarmed.)* But we're a team!

CACTUS: It has nothing to do with you. This detective biz isn't all it's cracked up to be. What if it's not worth it?

FRED: Not worth it? It's been great!

CACTUS: Has it?

FRED: We've only been here a year! Less than a year! You haven't even cleaned out the files from the previous occupant. We're still getting Marley's junk mail!

CACTUS: There was a time it felt exciting. I thought what we did here mattered. At least I hoped so.

FRED: Of course it matters. You're a private investigator!

CACTUS: Yeah, divorces, custody cases, professional Peeping Toms? How noble is that? All I do is track the broken bonds of love. No, Fred, I've learned too many ways to stick it to your friends and lovers in a double-cross.

FRED: It's not always like that.

CACTUS: Per day, plus expenses ... Fred, there's enough money to take a few months off, both of us, to think things through.

FRED: Think what? That you're crazy? I love my job. I love working with you.

CACTUS: Fred, there are other jobs ...

FRED: It's not just a job! And the lease! You've got to sign that lease! Sign it now, you can always break it later. Don't be in such a rush to close us down. Cactus, please think about the great cases we've had ...

CACTUS: Great cases?

FRED: Remember when you crawled through the massage parlor window? And when we found the stolen gold-plated you-know-what? How about The Great Moosehead Caper? You know, when you helped Gwendolyn Westlake steal her husband's moosehead right off the bedroom wall. And then the two of your buried it and sent him back a treasure map!

CACTUS: *(Laughs.)* We didn't steal anything. It was community property.

FRED: Well, then, what about Molly Spencer? You were the one who found her two kids after her ex-husband kidnapped them. The cops gave up on that case. But it was like a mission for you.

CACTUS: No one else would take it.

FRED: How could you think of giving all that up?

Cactus: How can you remember all that?

Fred: I type the files.

Cactus: Fred, I'm trying to be serious.

Fred: *(Imitating a tough-guy detective.)* But, Sweetheart, you told me that you wanted to be a private detective ever since you were a little kid.

Cactus: Yeah. A private eye. A fedora, a trenchcoat and a gun. That trusty piece of iron you always keep by your side. Following your instinct over your good sense. A solitary soldier seeking justice. Ha! I was 12 when I told Sister Marguerite I was going to be a detective just like Mike Hammer on the TV. She was impressed. She suggested that maybe I needed more prayer.

Fred: I think you need some now. *(HE pauses.)* Oh God, don't let her do this! Why don't you sign the lease? Here. Now.

Cactus: Fred. I haven't done anything yet.

Fred: I know. Sign. Cactus, you can't really see yourself doing something else?

(CACTUS goes to the window and opens it. The SAXOPHONE is playing "Deck the Halls.")

Cactus: I'm trying. I don't know, I've got to think.

Fred: It's cold out there.

Cactus: I think better on the fire escape. Where I can listen to Tommy's sax.

(SHE begins to climb out.)

Fred: *(HE waves the lease at her again.)* You can't open the windows in just any office, you know. They don't let you have your own fire escape and meditation area.

(STUART WINDSOR walks through the door, whistling "Deck the Halls" along with the SAX. HE holds a large package in his hands. WINDSOR cuts a dashing picture. HE is a man who wears clothes well, and HE walks into the office wearing a tuxedo. WINDSOR is more than a bit too formal for the surroundings. CACTUS is half-way out the window.)

WINDSOR: Running away?

(Startled, CACTUS bangs her head on the window and is further irritated.)

CACTUS: Stuart!
WINDSOR: That's me.
CACTUS: You're the last person I expected to see here tonight. *(SHE looks to FRED for help.)* Uh, Fred ...
FRED: Oh no, I can't watch. *(Heads for the door.)* I left something down the hall. I'll just be a minute ...
WINDSOR: Awfully nice of you, Fred. This is personal.
CACTUS: It's not going to be personal.
FRED: *(To CACTUS.)* Don't do anything radical.

(FRED exits.)

WINDSOR: Don't you ever lock the doors? Or windows?
CACTUS: *(CACTUS assesses his attire.)* We don't stand on formality here.

WINDSOR: Formality has nothing to do with burglary.

CACTUS: Don't worry, they never steal anything.

WINDSOR: So I heard. What's so interesting out there?

CACTUS: Just ... a little saxophone music. What's on your mind?

WINDSOR: No time for pleasantries? I brought you a present.

CACTUS: A king bearing gifts, or just a deputy king? *(WINDSOR reveals a large plant in his package. SHE softens slightly.)* A Christmas Cactus! Where on earth did you find it? I thought every florist in town was sold out!

WINDSOR: I have my resources. I know it's your favorite. Zygocactus Truncatus. I looked it up. I know lots of things you like.

CACTUS: I hate that about you, Stuart. But thank you ... for the plant. *(SHE sets it down and admires it.)* Anything else on your mind? DA business?

WINDSOR: And ... Merry Christmas.

CACTUS: Merry Christmas. And?

WINDSOR: Merry Christmas ... And ... Happy New Year.

CACTUS: Stuart, what's up?

WINDSOR: You tell me, Cactus. Rumor has it you haven't signed your lease renewal yet.

CACTUS: Hey! Did someone put out a press release?

WINDSOR: If it makes any difference, I approve. This isn't exactly the safest neighborhood.

CACTUS: It's safe enough.

WINDSOR: So that's why you had a break-in?

CACTUS: They had the wrong address! Lay off!

WINDSOR: You know you could always go to work for the DA's office, as an investigator. The offer's open. Of course you've always ignored my advice. But it is a good salary. It

A CHRISTMAS CACTUS

would be worth your while. We could work together. You could do something about that car.

CACTUS: Leave my car out of this.

WINDSOR: It's an eyesore.

CACTUS: It's a classic.

WINDSOR: A '62 Plymouth is not a classic, it's just too ugly to die. It's too ugly to steal ... Cactus, let's not argue. Besides, if you really wanted a change ... you could go back to law school.

CACTUS: Law school!

WINDSOR: Don't forget, I knew you when you were just Katie Bridget O'Riley. When you were interested in justice.

CACTUS: I still am. That's why I dropped out of law school. You're so tied up in the letter of the law, you wouldn't know justice if it mugged you in a blind alley.

WINDSOR: You're being unfair, Katie.

CACTUS: It's Cactus.

WINDSOR: Ah yes. Prickly, but pretty. I think you'd be a great attorney.

CACTUS: Now you insult me.

WINDSOR: Cactus, please. I'm doing my darndest to be nice. Some people think I'm a charming guy.

CACTUS: That's what they say in the papers. It must be true.

WINDSOR: I sent you a Christmas card.

CACTUS: You sent half the city a Christmas card. Which one was it? *(SHE selects one of the cards.)* Ah yes, Santa in court. You'll go far, Counselor.

WINDSOR: *(Determined to be cheerful.)* I'm trying! Cactus, let's start over. Think about it. Why don't you come out with me, tonight?

CACTUS: What?!

WINDSOR: To the Mayor's Christmas Ball.

CACTUS: I should have known that's why you look like a magazine cover.

WINDSOR: You really think so?

CACTUS: Yeah, sometimes you only look like a shirt ad.

WINDSOR: I understand there'll be a lot of media there. Come with me.

CACTUS: Me? Go with you? To the fanciest affair in town? Tonight? On five minutes notice?

WINDSOR: It would be fun. Kind of spontaneous, you know?

CACTUS: Spontaneous! Dressed like this?

WINDSOR: You look wonderful! Don't worry about it. People show up in just anything ...

CACTUS: Now I'm wearing just anything.

WINDSOR: Wait, you don't understand. I really meant to call you earlier.

CACTUS: You planned a surprise attack?

WINDSOR: Sort of ...

CACTUS: I'm not good enough to call up for a regular date, but you think nothing of parading me around a black-tie ball like you just dragged me in off the street!

WINDSOR: That's not what I meant! I *wanted* to call you. I meant to call you. But that never works. You always say no or back out because you say you don't like to plan anything! I know we've had our differences in the past, but the new year is right around the corner, we could start over again. Be friends ... We were friends once ...

CACTUS: I have this quirk. I have to like my friends.

WINDSOR: It seems to me what you're really trying to say is...

CACTUS: I know what I'm saying! Don't you dare tell me

what I'm saying!
WINDSOR: I didn't mean ...
CACTUS: You do that all the time, you bully.

(SHE advances on him, grabbing a letter opener from the desk.)

WINDSOR: Now, Cactus.
CACTUS: Courtroom tactics! That just really drives me crazy. It does. I'm dangerous when I feel crazy!
WINDSOR: But very attractive.

(WINDSOR bobs away from her.)

CACTUS: Go away! I have plans. I have a party to go to.
WINDSOR: A party?
CACTUS: A party. Not your kind, of course ... So go schmooze with the Mayor. Smile for the cameras. Please, leave me in peace. It's the season for peace.
WINDSOR: I know what's wrong. You're still moping over that old boyfriend.
CACTUS: He is none of your business.
WINDSOR: It's all over, huh? I thought so.
CACTUS: You know, Stuart, you ought to try blondes. You know, "Body by Fisher, Brains by Tinker."
WINDSOR: I prefer redheads. Besides, I'll grow on you. I can wait.

(CACTUS glares back.)

CACTUS: Well, at least you're dressed for the job.

(CACTUS opens the door for him.)

Windsor: Would you like to tell me why so many of our conversations end this way?
Cactus: Merry Christmas, Counselor.
Windsor: *(Sighs.)* I'll be back. I don't know why, but ... I will.

(WINDSOR exits. CACTUS picks darts off the dartboard, steps back and starts throwing them viciously at the board. In a few moments, FRED returns. HE enters cautiously.)

Cactus: Law school. Law school!
Fred: The part I like best is how he always makes you feel so good.
Cactus: That man!
Fred: What did he do?
Cactus: He told me I could work at the DA's office.
Fred: *(Delighted.)* No! The swine.
Cactus: Then, he wanted to drag me off with him to the Mayor's Christmas Ball!
Fred: The black-tie affair at the Skyline Room? What an insult.
Cactus: No invitation. No notice. No time to dress! I think he actually thought I'd go for it!
Fred: A miscalculation.
Cactus: He's used to women fawning all over him. Well, I don't do that.
Fred: It wouldn't be any fun to work for him anyway. You couldn't boss people around the way you like to.
Cactus: Aren't you supposed to go home?

(There is a commotion outside the office door. Two men burst into the room: NEVILLE SMEDLEY and RAMON RAMIREZ. SMEDLEY is in a state of near-hysterical desperation. RAMON seems very uncomfortable. SMEDLEY holds a gun on them but doesn't seem at ease with it. SAXOPHONE MUSIC drifts up, to the tune of "Hark! The Herald Angels Sing.")

FRED: May I help you?
SMEDLEY: Okay, everybody freeze!
CACTUS: The office is closed.
SMEDLEY: Can it. I got a score to settle up with the occupants of this office.
FRED: I handle all the accounting here.
SMEDLEY: Shut up. My name is Smedley. Mean anything to you?
FRED: Perhaps in our files.

(FRED moves to the cabinet.)

SMEDLEY: Hold it!
CACTUS: Smedley? Do I know you?
SMEDLEY: And this is Ramirez.
RAMON: *(RAMON walks toward them, shakes hands with FRED, and apologizes to CACTUS.)* Ramon Ramirez. I am pleased to meet you. I am very sorry for this intrusion.
CACTUS: Fred, check out their ensembles. No doubt designed at the city jail.
SMEDLEY: Our tuxedos are at the cleaners. But I got other things on my mind.
CACTUS: There's obviously some mistake. I don't know you.

SMEDLEY: Cut it! Where is he?

CACTUS: I think you'd better go.

SMEDLEY: Not till your boss shows up. We've got things to talk about.

CACTUS: Excuse me? What *boss*?

SMEDLEY: *(Waves the gun wildly.)* The sleazeball who sent me to jail!

(CACTUS looks at FRED and shakes her head.)

CACTUS: I'm the boss here, Smedley. And stop waving that thing around.

SMEDLEY: Don't give me that crap. Marley! Where's Marley?

CACTUS: Jake Marley?

RAMON: Yes, Señor Jake Marley.

SMEDLEY: *(Shaking the gun.)* You heard me!

CACTUS: Marley is dead.

RAMON: Muerto?

SMEDLEY: He can't be dead. I'm going to kill him.

RAMON: But you said nothing about killing! Madre de Dios, not on Christmas!

CACTUS: You're too late. He died in his sleep ...

SMEDLEY: You're lying.

CACTUS: Just a year ago.

SMEDLEY: *(Getting more upset.)* He's not here?

CACTUS: The name on the door is O'Riley.

(RAMON opens the door to take a look.)

RAMON: She is right! The name is O'Riley.

A CHRISTMAS CACTUS

SMEDLEY: Christ! Marley dead? No! It can't be. You're saying he got the drop on me again!

CACTUS: Marley is dead. I've got the office now. Sorry.

SMEDLEY: *(Shaken.)* But I dreamed about this ... I worked it out, every day, every single day in that stinking hole. Marley's the guy who gave them phony evidence. I spend two years in jail, and now he's dead?

CACTUS: The guy was a detective. If he put you away, maybe he was just doing his job.

SMEDLEY: It was a frame! And Marley knows it.

RAMON: Señor Smedley, it is no good. You cannot get revenge on a man who is dead. To try is to make your soul sick. We should go.

SMEDLEY: *(HE paces, thinking.)* I'm thinking! There's got to be some way to prove I didn't do it. I can't go back. I won't go back. I didn't steal that money. I was set up.

FRED: What money?

CACTUS: Innocent men don't usually carry an arsenal around.

SMEDLEY: I was innocent, and they put me in jail.

RAMON: The world is full of paradox. I was there too.

CACTUS: Two innocent guys. So I've noticed. Look, Smedley, I don't know you, you don't know me. We could say you got the wrong office. We could say I never saw you.

SMEDLEY: Yeah, we could say that ... And we could say I've got ... Christmas cookies for brains. The second I'm out of here, you call the cops.

CACTUS: It's Christmas. I'll give you an hour.

SMEDLEY: No good, Red. That doesn't solve my problem. No, I've got a better idea. You. You're a private eye? A woman dick?

CACTUS: That's right.

SMEDLEY: *(To FRED.)* And who are you?

FRED: I'm Ms. O'Riley's associate. *(CACTUS gives him a look.)* Uh, executive secretary.

SMEDLEY: *(HE shakes his head, then turns to CACTUS. HE shrugs.)* Are you any good?

CACTUS: Why, are you comparison shopping?

SMEDLEY: *(Waving the gun at her.)* You better be good, 'cause I'm gonna hire you, Red. Starting now. I know they stole the money and framed me. I been thinking about it for a long time. So all you got to do is find it.

CACTUS: Wait a minute ...

RAMON: *(To SMEDLEY.)* If this man is dead, he can do nothing for me. I must find Teresa, my friend. The city is so big ...

SMEDLEY: Someone's got to do this. "Innocence must be vindicated." I read that in a book.

RAMON: What book was that? I'd like to know. We should always improve ourselves.

SMEDLEY: What I'm saying is just stay here for now, Ramon, then we can take care of your problem. Please.

RAMON: These streets look familiar to me. I am close to the barrio.

CACTUS: This is ridiculous!

SMEDLEY: Don't worry, I'll pay you. You know. Later.

CACTUS: Triple fees for fugitives!

SMEDLEY: Triple?!

FRED: That'll be a nice chunk of change.

CACTUS: And I don't work very well at gunpoint.

SMEDLEY: The gun stays until we establish some rules here. No one leaves till we find it.

A CHRISTMAS CACTUS

CACTUS: Find what?!
SMEDLEY: Evidence. Real evidence.
FRED: No problem. It's probably filed under E.

(FRED heads toward the files, but stops as SMEDLEY waves the gun.)

CACTUS: Suppose you tell me who you are, where you came from, and what you want.

SMEDLEY: All right. But you gotta understand. I didn't do anything wrong. I don't want to hurt anyone. But this is serious.

CACTUS: Smedley, Neville Smedley ...

SMEDLEY: Neville F. Smedley

CACTUS: What's the "F" for?

SMEDLEY: Fezziwig. Want to make something of it?

CACTUS: Not necessarily. I remember you now. You embezzled a million dollars from the Handicapped Children's Fund ...

FRED: Two million! I remember the headlines. "Millions Missing From Tiny Tim Fund."

CACTUS: That money was never recovered ...

SMEDLEY: Don't start on me, Red. I didn't do it and you're going to prove that.

CACTUS: How am I supposed to do that?

SMEDLEY: You're the detective!

CACTUS: You had a trial!

SMEDLEY: You ever gone through that? I didn't know what to do. I was shook. Railroaded. I think in numbers, not people.

CACTUS: Weren't you some sort of low-level politician?

SMEDLEY: What do you mean "low-level"? I was the assistant to the City Clerk, in charge of bookkeeping. Maybe it doesn't sound like much to you, but it was my career. My life. Only ...

CACTUS: Only what?

SMEDLEY: Someone decided I'd be the fall guy for this scheme. Figured I was too stupid to know until it was too late. You gotta believe me ...

(HE waves his gun for emphasis.)

CACTUS: I'm thinking about it.

FRED: We're thinking hard. We need to set up a contract.

RAMON: It's good you are thinking of the details.

CACTUS: Get the standard ... we'll amend it as we go along. *(FRED takes a contract from a file drawer. CACTUS retrieves a tape recorder and turns it on. SHE speaks into it, checks her watch.)* This is Cactus O'Riley, December 24, at 5:20 p.m. I was closing the office, O'Riley Consulting, when an intrusion prevented ...

SMEDLEY: Intrusion? I'm not an intrusion!

CACTUS: The speaker is Neville F. Smedley. Just tell the story, Smedley...

SMEDLEY: Okay. One day there I was, working, paying taxes. The next thing I know I'm arrested, two million dollars is missing from these handicapped kids. I get a jerk lawyer from the public defender. Marley shows up at the trial and gives them all this phony evidence saying I did it.

CACTUS: He was a detective! His job was to detect. *(CACTUS fumbles with the tape recorder.)* Fred, take notes.

FRED: Is technology rearing its ugly head again?

A CHRISTMAS CACTUS

CACTUS: By the way, Smedley, did you steal the funds?

SMEDLEY: Would I be here if I had a million dollars stashed someplace?

CACTUS: Revenge is always a good reason.

RAMON: No, revenge is a bad reason. But justice is a good reason.

SMEDLEY: I didn't know Jake Marley from John Doe. If he didn't frame me, then someone set him up, too. All I've been living for was to get to Marley and ask him why, why me?

CACTUS: If you were the accountant, why didn't you figure it out then?

SMEDLEY: I was just a bookkeeper, not a CPA, for crying out loud. I was in shock. They kept giving me these little white pills to calm me down.

CACTUS: So what was this plan?

SMEDLEY: The Tiny Tim Fund was designed to finance an $11 million dollar construction project for a new wing of the Children's Hospital. But it was set up with a $2 million kickback. Built in from the beginning. That's the way I figure it. All they needed was a patsy, just in case someone noticed that all the money was filtering out.

CACTUS: You.

RAMON: Would a guilty man be so upset? You should listen.

CACTUS: And why should I listen to you?

RAMON: Because I am an honest man.

CACTUS: Looks like we're all just a bunch of honest shmoes. So who are they? Who's guilty?

SMEDLEY: I think maybe the Mayor. And the contractors, Sawdust Construction.

CACTUS: *(SHE clicks off the tape and smiles.)* The Mayor?

Always high on my list of culprits. Know him? Keep writing, Fred, you know I hate these things.

SMEDLEY: Well, not personally. I shook his hand a couple of times.

CACTUS: Fred. If we were going to believe all this ... If Smedley or anyone were nailed in a frame, of course there'd be no visible connection to trace back to the Mayor, unlike the rest of Hizzoner's crooked cronies.

SMEDLEY: What I hated most was reading all the papers. They kept saying it was such a devious scheme and I didn't have a clue what they were talking about.

CACTUS: *(Shrugs.)* Now, tell me *how* he did it.

SMEDLEY: I wish I knew. Somehow, all these checks were cashed, none of the names on the checks existed, but my name was all over every order.

FRED: That sounds like a real mess.

CACTUS: How'd you get here, Smedley?

SMEDLEY: They were taking me to the dentist on the jail bus. Got a bad filling. Right back here. *(Points.)* There was an accident.

RAMON: A miraculous accident. That's how we met.

SMEDLEY: That's right.

CACTUS: Where'd you get the gun?

SMEDLEY: *(Embarrassed.)* The bus smashed into a pawnshop. I grabbed it out of the window. *(Uncertainly.)* But I know how to use it! I do!

(FRED and CACTUS exchange looks.)

RAMON: I never thought the gun was a good idea.

SMEDLEY: How often do you get that kind of chance? I

wound up here. All I wanted to do was get the truth out of Marley.

CACTUS: I can see you're a real tough guy, a real killer.

RAMON: He is not a killer! He's not a bad hombre.

SMEDLEY: *(Upset.)* I know, I'm no killer. But I'm no embezzler either. And now, I'm a lousy fugitive ... I was a model prisoner, though.

(SMEDLEY absentmindedly picks up a cookie and starts munching on it. The gun is still in the other hand. Up from the street below come SAXOPHONE strains of "God Rest Ye Merry, Gentlemen." RAMON goes over to the window and looks out. FRED keeps his eye on RAMON.)

RAMON: That man down there. Playing music. Who is he?

FRED: Tommy. Everyone in the neighborhood knows him.

RAMON: He plays here often?

FRED: Almost every night.

RAMON: I remember this man.

CACTUS: So, the whole city's probably crawling with cops looking for you.

SMEDLEY: I guess. What does it matter? The opportunity presented itself ... Seemed like a good idea at the time.

RAMON: *(Drawing CACTUS aside.)* Señorita Cactus, I must speak to you, please. I know that Neville Smedley is a sincere man. And you must help him if you can. I believe it with my heart.

CACTUS: What are you talking about?

RAMON: When we were on the bus, I was praying very hard. I asked God for a sign that I would get to see my family again. My soul was very troubled.

CACTUS: A sign?

RAMON: There was a guard in the front of the bus and one in the back. They carry guns. The bus was going very fast. It turned over. There was a great flash of light in front of my eyes and I thought I would die. I looked up and the window was pushed out.

SMEDLEY: The emergency exit. We were right next to it.

RAMON: A miracle. I knew I must run. This man was the only other man who got out of the bus. *We* were given another chance. We are innocent. You cannot turn your back on a miracle.

(SMEDLEY looks at her expectantly.)

FRED: There's not much in our "miracle" file ...

CACTUS: Ramon, why were you in jail?

RAMON: They call it being an illegal alien. They were going to send me back. Smedley said that this man, Marley, could perhaps get me a green card. He said he would make him do it, if he could. But I have done nothing wrong!

CACTUS: It is illegal to cross the border without papers.

RAMON: Is it God's law or man's law?

CACTUS: Please, Ramon. No trick questions tonight. (*The phone RINGS. EVERYONE starts.*) Oh no. It's that woman!

SMEDLEY: A woman? Answer it.

FRED: *(HE answers on the speaker phone.)* O'Riley Consulting.

ADELAIDE: Frederick. This is your mother.

(EVERYONE can hear her voice.)

FRED: Adelaide, dear! How are you?

ADELAIDE: Don't "how are you" me, Frederick. You said you'd be home by now.

SMEDLEY: Who's this, your warden?

ADELAIDE: Who is that?

FRED: No one.

ADELAIDE: Fred, I warned you about working for that Cactus woman. Late on Christmas Eve of all nights. Just what kind of name is "Cactus" anyway?

CACTUS: I was named after the Saint! Mrs. Booker, something came up.

RAMON: *(Puzzled.)* There is no St. Cactus. Are you Catholic?

CACTUS: Occasionally.

ADELAIDE: You're having an office party. I thought so.

FRED: It's not exactly a party, Adelaide.

CACTUS: There's a case that's really got us tied up here.

FRED: Not quite tied up. But busy, very busy.

ADELAIDE: I'm coming right over there, now!

CACTUS: No. Mrs. Booker, you can't!

ADELAIDE: Just what kind of parties do you people throw? Are you so ashamed you don't want me there?

FRED: Adelaide, please. This is a delicate situation.

CACTUS: You don't understand. Trust me!

ADELAIDE: You want me to trust a person named Cactus! I could trust a person named Iris or Violet ... That would inspire a little confidence. Fred, are you sure you should be working for this woman anyway? *(Rattling on.)* Of course women can be detectives. I could have been a detective. If I wanted to. A detective should be dependable. There's Miss Marple, for example. Marple. That's a good solid name, why ...

(SMEDLEY abruptly slams down the phone.)

CACTUS: What did you do that for?
SMEDLEY: We've got work to do.
CACTUS: Well, she'll just call back. And back. And back.
SMEDLEY: Not if we disconnect the phone.

(HE unplugs it.)

CACTUS: Look, Smedley, I've got Marley's files around here. We'll see if there's a file on you, okay? We can make a trade. The gun! Give me the gun. Give me the gun! *(SMEDLEY hesitates.)* Make up your mind. I don't work for anybody as a hostage. But if you've got a case, you don't need the gun.

SMEDLEY: *(HE reluctantly hands it to her.)* Could we get to work on it now? Please?

CACTUS: *(SHE turns away and opens the gun to check. Satisfied, SHE tucks the gun into her waistband.)* Now. But I set the ground rules. I give you tonight, then you leave. If you're caught, you're on your own. I could lose a license here. And I've got damn little to go on, except you look like you'd make a lousy criminal.

SMEDLEY: It's a deal, Red.

CACTUS: Okay, now let's see what we've got. Fred, see if you can find a file on "Smedley," or "Handicapped Children's Fund." *(SHE heads for a file cabinet.)* I'll check these.

FRED: Or "Tiny Tim"?

SMEDLEY: Marley's files! That's great! You think they'll

clear me?

CACTUS: If someone framed you, it was a good job. We have to look for small things, inconsistencies. Chances are we won't find anything. The trail on this is dead cold.

SMEDLEY: But we have to find something.

CACTUS: Look. Marley didn't leave much, just a few files, a complete set of dusty old Dickens novels and this questionable object of art. My hat rack.

(SMEDLEY removes CACTUS's hat from the bust.)

SMEDLEY: It looks like Einstein.

FRED: *(Taking the hat back, HE puts it back on the statue.)* It's Charles Dickens and I don't want to hear anything more about it!

(RAMON examines the bust.)

RAMON: It is Charles Dickens. Born 1812, died 1870. A famous Victorian writer. He wrote with so much compassion.

CACTUS: This is a conspiracy, right?

RAMON: I was an English teacher at home. I studied 19th century English writers. Fascinating.

FRED: I'll get the files. Why don't you just make yourselves at home?

SMEDLEY: *(HE wanders over to the small Christmas tree.)* Hey, can you turn this thing on? *(FRED lights up the tree. SMEDLEY eats another cookie and looks at the tree.)* That's nice. It's been a long time since I've seen a tree. A real green one. I used to like Christmas. Before ...

FRED: *(FRED is looking through a box of old files.)* Here it is, and *(flipping through it)* it looks really complete.

SMEDLEY: *(HE takes it and sits down.)* Wow. Pretty thick. I didn't know it would be this thick.

(RAMON sighs deeply and turns away from them. HE walks over to the Christmas tree, HE picks up an ornament and stares at it. Another soft Christmas carol, "Away in a Manger," comes from the street.)

RAMON: Feliz Navidad. Por Dios! Teresita mia. Where are you on this night? How can I find you? The address I know, the city I do not. But you are close, you must be. *(CACTUS and FRED listen intently. RAMON carefully hangs the ornament.)* It is such a big country. Why do they care about one poor man? I would be the best American, if they let me.

FRED: Who is Teresa, Ramon?

RAMON: Mi esposa. She wasn't even there when they took me. She may not know what happened to me. There is no telephone. Who can I tell? Who can I trust?

CACTUS: Word travels on the street.

RAMON: I cannot risk her being deported too. I want my child born in this country.

CACTUS: She's pregnant?

RAMON: *(Nods.)* They arrested me during Las Posadas, the procession of the Holy Family. Sometimes I think there is no room for God, there is no room for us.

CACTUS: There's never been any room at the inn, Ramon. Fred, we sat up here and watched the Las Posadas procession.

RAMON: *(Excitedly.)* You saw it, from here? And that man, Tommy, he was playing here that night?

FRED: Yeah, I remember. He played while they sang.
CACTUS: That's right.
RAMON: Then I must stay here.
CACTUS: What about finding your wife?
RAMON: I will find her right here. There will be a procession later, to Midnight Mass. They will carry candles and sing again. She will be there in the street.
FRED: But won't they be out there looking for illegal aliens again?
RAMON: Don't you believe in miracles?
FRED: Well, I could certainly use one tonight. Or two ...
SMEDLEY: *(Reading the file, outraged.)* What a bunch of crap. It's lies, all lies!
CACTUS: Keep reading, Smedley. Ramon, what's she like, your Teresa?
RAMON: She is beautiful. Soft. Kind. She is like twilight. You can never really know her and you know her so well. If I could see her. But it is Christmas ... I have no present for her. I have been working, I was to be paid in time ... *(Pause.)* Teresa ... She has been saving money. Pennies and nickels and dimes in a glass jar. It is painful to me, but she is so happy that she can put this money aside to buy a gift for me.
CACTUS: Does she believe in miracles?
RAMON: She must. We have nothing else.
SMEDLEY: *(Still with the file.)* Oh my God. It all looks so ... real. I look guilty. Look at this: a copy of a purchase order for electrical work. This company doesn't exist.
FRED: *(Taking one of the papers from the file.)* But it looks like your signature.
SMEDLEY: It is my signature, but I don't know how they got it.

FRED: Forgery?

CACTUS: Not according to the handwriting expert's testimony, here.

SMEDLEY: Don't you believe me?

CACTUS: Instinct tells me you're not quite bright enough to be an embezzler.

FRED: "Instinct"?

SMEDLEY: You're right! I'm not! That's what I've been trying to tell you!

CACTUS: Let's see the file. *(CACTUS looks through it, taking a sheet from the file.)* Hmmm ... The case summary looks pretty bad. Is there anything funny about this?

FRED: I don't know what you mean. This is the best-looking file I've ever seen. Very impressive.

CACTUS: That's what I mean. Your files are beautiful. But look at this: all typed, no notes in pen, no doodling, no White-Out, no scraps of paper, no yellow stickies ...

FRED: Perfect. *(Pause.)* Too perfect?

CACTUS: Details. Details. Details! It looks like it was written to order. My God. *(Thunderstruck.)* It doesn't look real, unless Marley was some kind of neat freak, a compulsive little rascal. Okay, Smedley. Let's say I believe you, for now. Let's look this place over. Everything. The files, the closet ... Maybe there is something.

FRED: That's the spirit! I believe you, Smedley.

SMEDLEY: You do?

FRED: Sure, I can smell a phony file.

CACTUS: Fred, you've got to go home.

FRED: What?!

CACTUS: Adelaide is expecting you. She's probably getting frantic.

FRED: You can't be serious. I'm on this case too. You need me.

CACTUS: I'll be all right. *(SHE goes to her desk to put SMEDLEY's gun away.)* Go home to Adelaide.

FRED: But, but ... This is really something. Something big! I'm not going. I'm not going to miss all the fun.

CACTUS: Fun! Are you crazy?

FRED: This is my first shot at a case.

(While THEY argue, ADELAIDE walks in unnoticed and stares at them.)

SMEDLEY: No one goes anywhere. That's part of the deal.

CACTUS: It's only Fred.

ADELAIDE: What do you mean, "only Fred"?

(THEY turn to see ADELAIDE.)

FRED: Adelaide!

CACTUS: Mrs. Booker?

SMEDLEY: Who's this?

CACTUS: I thought the door was locked. Fred, lock the door. Please.

ADELAIDE: I wouldn't bother with that. Your parties aren't that exclusive. Not in this neighborhood. What kind of nonsense is going on here? Someone hung up the phone on me!

CACTUS: Mrs. Booker, something popped up unexpectedly here ...

ADELAIDE: I'm not interested in that. *(To FRED. SHE turns to her son, not noticing that CACTUS has a gun, which*

CACTUS now is stashing behind a big bow in the Christmas Cactus.) No one hangs up on your mother. You know I didn't raise you to be ...

FRED: Adelaide, this is not a good place for you.

ADELAIDE: I never thought it was particularly good for you either, but I let you make up your own mind about it.

CACTUS: Oh God.

ADELAIDE: It's about time he remembered God, isn't it?

RAMON: We were just talking about Him.

ADELAIDE: *(SHE looks at SMEDLEY. THEIR eyes lock.)* But who is this ... Fred?

FRED: Oh, well, it's ... a friend.

SMEDLEY: Smedley, Neville Smedley, ma'am.

(HE reaches out his hand.)

ADELAIDE: *(SHE shakes it.)* Adelaide Booker.

SMEDLEY: Adelaide, I'm ... I'm delighted to meet you.

ADELAIDE: Fred, you never told me about Mr. Smedley.

FRED: And this is Mr. Ramirez. Another friend.

RAMON: Mucho gusto.

ADELAIDE: Likewise, I'm sure. Fred, you've been pretty mysterious today, not telling me where we're going, now ... ?

(The SAXOPHONE plays "What Child Is This?")

CACTUS: Fred, why don't you take your mother home?

FRED: But Cactus ...

SMEDLEY: *(HE goes to the door and blocks it.)* No one leaves. We agreed. That's part of the deal.

ADELAIDE: Not till I have an explanation. And an apology.

A CHRISTMAS CACTUS

SMEDLEY: I'm sorry, Adelaide, Mrs. Booker. I can't let you go.

ADELAIDE: *(Confused.)* What? Why ever not?

SMEDLEY: Because that's the rules. Once you're in, you can't go till we find ... something.

CACTUS: No, Smedley. I make the rules, remember?

SMEDLEY: Are we playing a game here?

ADELAIDE: *(Intrigued.)* Game? Rules - what rules?

CACTUS: Shut up, Smedley. It's nothing, Adelaide.

RAMON: This is not a game. There are too many people already.

ADELAIDE: At a party on Christmas Eve? Don't be silly. There must be a good reason for me to stay.

FRED: You're imagining things, Adelaide.

ADELAIDE: No. Something's up, Frederick. I know what's going on here. Don't try to fool me. You hung up the phone on me because you knew that I would come right over. *(ADELAIDE walks around the office, rearranging an ornament on the tree and examining Christmas cards. SHE looks each person over.)* He says there are rules. *(To CACTUS.)* You say you made the rules. Where do we have rules? In games. You are playing a game. And I love games. Fred, it's a game, isn't it? You know how I love games! You did this for me, didn't you? I know what this is. *(Smiling.)* It's a murder mystery party, isn't it?

FRED: A murder mystery party?

RAMON: Please, no more talk of murder. It makes me nervous.

ADELAIDE: You never could fool me!

FRED: Exactly! *(HE catches CACTUS's look.)* Well ...

ADELAIDE: You know how I've been dying to go to one ...

So now you've arranged one. How delightful! But you know, I thought these parties were supposed to take place on a cruise ...

FRED: *(Weakly.)* A cruise?

ADELAIDE: Or in a mansion?

RAMON: This is not a mansion.

ADELAIDE: Of course a detective agency is even more clever! In a holiday setting. I'm mad for it. Fred, I never dreamed you'd go to all this trouble for your mother.

FRED: Neither did I.

CACTUS: This is getting out of hand. *(SHE picks up FRED's coat and hands it to him. SHE starts pushing him and ADELAIDE out the door.)* Nothing is going on. You're leaving now. Thanks for stopping by. Merry Christmas.

ADELAIDE: *(Taking off her coat.)* It's the newest thing. All my friends have been to a murder mystery party. Everyone except me. But this is so much more original. I mean, everyone else knew about theirs weeks in advance. Fred, what a lovely Christmas present!

FRED: *(Helplessly.)* Just a small part of it, dear.

ADELAIDE: And the guests you're expecting tomorrow, it's all a ruse, isn't it?

FRED: No, tomorrow is real. Tonight's the charade.

(Outside the office a police SIREN is heard. Flashing red lights are reflected in the office. CACTUS and SMEDLEY run to the window. THEY are followed by the others. The SIREN stops, but the red light keeps flashing.)

SMEDLEY: Holy Smokes! I got a feeling they're looking for us. Ramon and me.

A CHRISTMAS CACTUS

RAMON: They are getting out of the car. Por Dios.

CACTUS: They're just conducting a foot search through the alley.

ADELAIDE: They're looking for you? This is too perfect. I'm so happy.

RAMON: We must hide. We must run.

SMEDLEY: We got nowhere to run, friend.

ADELAIDE: Do you suppose they'll come up here? Maybe if we wave ...

RAMON: They can't find us! They can't come up here.

ADELAIDE: They can't?

SMEDLEY: You don't want us to go back to jail do you?

ADELAIDE: Well, no! Certainly not before the game is over.

(CACTUS steers ADELAIDE away from the window.)

CACTUS: They're for atmosphere, Adelaide.

ADELAIDE: I understand. You're been very thorough, Fred.

CACTUS: Yes, Fred, very thorough. Such a detail man. *(A loud KNOCK at the door. OFFSTAGE: "Police. We'd like to talk with you.")* Quick, give me the cookies. *(The cookie platter is passed over to her. SHE opens the door and walks out.)* Merry Christmas, officers!

(ADELAIDE walks to the door and peers out.)

ADELAIDE: It's a lovely party! Won't you come in? No? Well, maybe later.

CACTUS: *(Returning, minus some cookies.)* Seems there's some silly little A.P.B. alert. They're too busy to join the "party."

ADELAIDE: When I came over, I must confess, I didn't know what kind of ... *party* you were having. I thought it would be one of those awful drunken office parties that tacky people have on Christmas. I had no idea it was for me! *(ADELAIDE reaches for a cookie, then hesitates.)* They're not poison, are they?

RAMON: Poison? You think this nice Cactus would poison the food? That she would poison those policemen? Dios!

ADELAIDE: My friend Julia went to one of these parties and ate some hors d'oeuvres. Then they told her they were the poison ones that the victim ate. And she had to be dead until the evening was over. She was so disappointed.

FRED: We think poison's been overdone.

CACTUS: Not necessarily. I wish we had thought of it. *(Throwing FRED a look.)* But these are just real. Help yourself.

ADELAIDE: When is the detective coming? I know that's a part of it.

CACTUS: I'm the detective, Adelaide! Keep that in mind, why don't you. We all have our little parts to play in this charade.

ADELAIDE: Good. I can't wait.

FRED: Yes, as a matter of fact, Mr. Ramirez is an undercover policeman ...

ADELAIDE: Let me see. *(Gesturing at RAMON.)* He looks just like a ... a ...

RAMON: *(Alarmed.)* What do I look like?

ADELAIDE: A gardener?

RAMON: A gardener? At a detective agency on Christmas Eve?

ADELAIDE: I don't know. But you're really an undercover

policeman dressed like a gardener, so I suppose that's a clue. And you're ethnic too, aren't you? Well, my mind is racing.

CACTUS: Fred!

FRED: *(Whispering.)* I've always wanted to lie to my mother.

CACTUS: We don't need this to get too complicated.

FRED: She's off and running.

ADELAIDE: Gardener ... Earl Stanley Gardner! The writer! Is it one of his mysteries? I know them all! Is it *The Case of the Guilty Gravedigger*?

CACTUS: No, Adelaide. But close.

ADELAIDE: Well, it's just a guess. *Murder in the Mortuary*?

RAMON: This miracle is taking a long time.

CACTUS: It's a game. You have to pretend. Like acting.

SMEDLEY: I think you're doing fine, Adelaide.

RAMON: Is this what gringos do on Christmas Eve? We go to church!

ADELAIDE: You're an actor! Fred, you've gone to so much trouble. Mr. Ramirez, tell me what it's really like. It's so romantic. Playing a role, travelling ...

RAMON: I have studied with the best. El teatro ... *The Theatre of the Immigrant.*

CACTUS: Let's say that Mr. Ramirez is an illegal alien.

ADELAIDE: And he's so good for the part.

RAMON: Thank you. I am a ... a ... como se dice ... chameleon - night and day - I could be Juan Lopez, a cowboy from El Paso, or Pedro Gonzalez, who owns a restaurant. Or today, I am an undercover policeman posing as a gardener, Lt. Joe Hernandez. Is that right? This theatre is very exacting. One bad performance and you're on the first bus out of town.

ADELAIDE: Is it hard to get in this group?

(RAMON smiles and shrugs.) It must be as hard as the Stanislavski Method. I've heard about that.

RAMON: Similar. You must live the part.

ADELAIDE: Do you have an Equity card?

RAMON: No. The card I need is green.

ADELAIDE: I'm sure you'll make it. You're very talented.

(RAMON bows to her. The red lights of the police car fade away. CACTUS goes to the window.)

CACTUS: They're pulling out.

FRED: Guess they didn't find anything.

CACTUS: For now, anyway. Let's wrap this up.

ADELAIDE: Don't be silly, we're just getting started.

FRED: *(HE speaks quietly to CACTUS, who glares.)* Come on, it's her Christmas present.

ADELAIDE: *(To SMEDLEY.)* Isn't this fun? Are you a gardener too?

SMEDLEY: *(Dejectedly.)* No, I'm a con. I used to be a bookkeeper. Now I'm a fugitive.

ADELAIDE: Oh. A con man, I like that.

SMEDLEY: Not a con man, a convict! But I'm innocent. And nobody believes me.

ADELAIDE: I believe you! Anyone could see that. You have that look of oppressed innocence. But I'm sure with some good home cooking and a little attention, you'd just blossom. Just look at Fred.

SMEDLEY: Home cooking? I would blossom. I know I would!

ADELAIDE: What part can I play? I've got it, a gun moll! Could I be your gun moll?

A CHRISTMAS CACTUS

SMEDLEY: You could be my anything. *(Trying to act tough.)* Baby.

CACTUS: Smedley!

FRED: Mother! I mean, Adelaide!

ADELAIDE: For heaven's sakes, Fred. It's only a game.

CACTUS: That's right, only a game.

ADELAIDE: *(To SMEDLEY.)* Do you have a gun I can keep for you?

CACTUS: No guns, Mrs. Booker! Rules.

SMEDLEY: Uh, I had one. I traded it in. I hope I got a good deal.

ADELAIDE: I see. Well, it's better not to get caught with one. Did you wipe your prints off?

SMEDLEY: I didn't think about it.

CACTUS: A career criminal, no doubt.

ADELAIDE: Oh, that is going to look bad! We're in deep trouble.

SMEDLEY: That's what I'm afraid of.

ADELAIDE: By the way, who's dead?

SMEDLEY: Marley's dead.

CACTUS: Jake Marley. He was the detective who had this office before us.

ADELAIDE: Oh, I see. How did he die?

CACTUS: The possibilities are endless. He was such a detail man.

FRED: Marley died in his sleep. Of natural causes, they say.

ADELAIDE: Oh Fred, that's what they always say! First we have to prove he was murdered. Then you *know* the killer must be one of us here! And now we've got to find out who had the strongest motive for his demise.

CACTUS: I'm so glad you're so up on these mystery parties,

Adelaide. Motives and all. However, while we do that, we're looking for something, some ...

ADELAIDE: Clue.

FRED: Right. That would prove Mr. Smedley was framed.

CACTUS: By Jake Marley. But Marley was "killed" after Smedley was framed. *(SHE really thinks about it for a minute.)* Let's say Marley was a middle man. Whoever he was working for could have bumped him off.

SMEDLEY: Jeez, you think?

ADELAIDE: No! He framed Mr. Smedley?

SMEDLEY: Yes! Marley testified against me.

ADELAIDE: But Mr. Smedley's just a dear little man!

FRED: A dear little man?

ADELAIDE: He didn't even think about his fingerprints.

CACTUS: We're looking at everything here in a new light.

ADELAIDE: *(Knowingly.)* Of course. Whatever it is, it could be right under our noses.

CACTUS: Fred, I gotta think.

(CACTUS goes to the window and opens it.)

FRED: Wait, I'm coming.

SMEDLEY: Hey, the rules ...

CACTUS: We're not going anywhere. I think better on the fire escape. Besides, I want to see if that cruiser's still in the neighborhood.

ADELAIDE: We can't take any chances. We've got to keep this under wraps.

RAMON: *(To SMEDLEY.)* I will keep watch. And I want to look closer at this street.

ADELAIDE: Good. That will give me a few minutes to collect

my thoughts. I'm going to sit right here and just soak in the atmosphere. It sharpens my intuition so.

CACTUS: *(Looking at FRED, who's followed her.)* What is this?

FRED: A group effort.

SMEDLEY: You got five minutes.

(The THREE of them crawl out on the fire escape again. The SAXOPHONE plays "We Three Kings of Orient Ave.")

CACTUS: Give me some space! Don't draw any attention.

(During the following action, in the office, on the fire escape and in the street below, the lights come up on the individual scenes. Lights now spot the office with ADELAIDE and SMEDLEY. ADELAIDE gets her purse and fishes a large notebook out of it.)

SMEDLEY: What's that?

ADELAIDE: I just thought I'd make some notes. If I list all the characters and what we have so far, then I can jot down some thoughts and figure it all out.

SMEDLEY: Really?

ADELAIDE: Oh yes. I belong to the Mystery Book of the Month Club. Reading about crime is so relaxing, don't you think?

SMEDLEY: Maybe in other circumstances.

ADELAIDE: Anyway, I like to make lists of all the characters, their motives and where they were at the time of the crime. Oh, and lots of other things. It's silly, but it amuses me.

SMEDLEY: I like lists too. Ledgers. Nice straight columns ...

bottom lines. I appreciate a good list ... Mrs. Booker? I was wondering, is there a Mr. Booker? Is he likely to show up here too?

ADELAIDE: *(Breezily.)* Oh no, he's been dead for years. It's just been Fred and me. All alone. You know, if we're going to be a team, maybe you should call me Adelaide.

SMEDLEY: Yes, Adelaide. And ... I'm Neville.

ADELAIDE: What's that you're looking at?

SMEDLEY: *(Dejectedly.)* My file.

ADELAIDE: They've gathered a whole file on you? Ooh, can I see?

(SHE reaches out for it.)

SMEDLEY: *(Holding it back.)* I didn't do it, you know. This is just lies. I was framed.

ADELAIDE: That's good. Still in character. If I'm going to be your gun moll, you'd better tell me about yourself. *(SHE grabs the file.)* After all, I'm on your side. That's what a gun moll does, she keeps track of your gun, your enemies, your aliases, that sort of thing. And keep you company, of course. Even tough guys need company.

SMEDLEY: *(Sincerely.)* I'm not always such a tough guy. It's something I've had to learn.

ADELAIDE: *(Writing.)* "Not really a tough guy."

SMEDLEY: It's very scary in jail, especially if your credentials aren't up to par.

ADELAIDE: *(Writing.)* "Credentials." What kind of credentials?

SMEDLEY: Crimes have a certain status. Being convicted of embezzling is not a status crime, not where I am. It's

A CHRISTMAS CACTUS

downright embarrassing.

ADELAIDE: If you could choose your crime, what would it be?

SMEDLEY: I guess I'd be a ... a ... kissing bandit. *(HE kisses her cheek, then blushes.)* I'm sorry. I don't know why I did that.

ADELAIDE: Neville! Why, you're a romantic underneath it all, aren't you? I guess we all are.

SMEDLEY: I don't think I've ever met anyone like you, Adelaide.

ADELAIDE: Count on it.

(Lights dim on the office, and come up on the street below, with a soft light on the fire escape, revealing only CACTUS. FRED and RAMON remain in shadows. WINDSOR has come from Rivers Cafe, where he has downed a few drinks. Slightly inebriated, a little rumpled, his tie loose, HE is placed either on stage or in the audience, playing his role in the "street." HE gazes toward CACTUS's office. To his surprise, HE sees her on the fire escape, lit up in the night sky. Unaware that RAMON and FRED are also up there, WINDSOR rhapsodizes alone, romantically.)

WINDSOR: I don't understand. What'd I do wrong? The Mayor's Ball is a big deal. I thought she'd love it. She likes spur-of-the-moment adventures. I planned it for weeks. Cactus! *(Puzzled.)* What's she doing up there on the fire escape? You really know how to pick 'em, don't you? I've watched 'em come and go. Your boyfriend's gone now. Why do you love such losers? Under this tuxedo I have the soul of a lover. I know what I should do, Cactus. I know what you like. I should pretend I'm actually broke. In my spare time, I write avant-garde poetry about redheads and I paint ... badly. *(Resigned.)* But what's the use? You hate guys like me. Forgive me. I'm a lawyer. A successful lawyer. Is that a crime? You know, you'd make a damn fine lawyer. Well, you'd probably spend a fair amount of time in contempt of court. *(HE sings.)* "... my sweet contemptible you ..." Katie. Katie Bridget O'Riley ... Cactus! Who named you that? I have half a mind to ask.

(Focus returns to fire escape.)

CACTUS: There's nothing out here. What are you doing?
FRED: *(FRED peers through the window trying to see what's going on inside.)* They're getting along! Wow. No one gets along with Adelaide. *(HE turns back, viewing the street.)* Great view, huh. You could really watch the procession from here.
CACTUS: She'll be there, won't she? Teresa?
RAMON: Yes, and perhaps ...
CACTUS: We'll work on it. Oh no!

(SHE sees WINDSOR.)

FRED: What?
CACTUS: *(Whispering.)* It's Stuart. Shh. Maybe he won't notice.

(Depending on the staging limitations, the audience does not necessarily have to see WINDSOR during the following

exchange: They could simply hear his voice.)

WINDSOR: Cactus, is that you?
CACTUS: I don't believe this.
WINDSOR: I want to talk to you.
FRED: He's supposed to be at the ball!
WINDSOR: What are you doing?
CACTUS: What does it look like?
WINDSOR: Like you're out on the fire escape ... *(Noticing FRED.)* Out there with some guy!
FRED: *(HE steps into the light.)* I'm not just another guy.
WINDSOR: Fred! Your secretary?
CACTUS: Stuart, what are you doing here?
WINDSOR: Just in the neighborhood.
CACTUS: Have you been drinking?
WINDSOR: *(Drunkenly.)* I don't drink. O'Riley, are you having an affair with your secretary?
CACTUS: Oh, Stuart, please go home.
FRED: Wait a minute ...
WINDSOR: That's so tawdry. Never handle the help. A rule we follow at the DA's office.
CACTUS: Nothing is going on here! And leave the DA out of this!
FRED: We'll be the talk of the town. I like that.
RAMON: *(Alarmed.)* Is this man with the law?
CACTUS: This is a bad idea. We better get inside, guys.
WINDSOR: Another guy? You got *two* guys up there?
CACTUS: Don't be ridiculous. He's the maintenance man. This is a security check. The window lock was loose.
WINDSOR: On Christmas Eve?
CACTUS: You just told me we got lousy security in this

building. I took your words to heart.

RAMON: *(RAMON rattles the window and sizes up the framing. HE calls to WINDSOR..)* There's nothing wrong with this window. Everything is A-OK.

CACTUS: Good job, it certainly looks sturdy. It's cold out here, go on inside. *(FRED and RAMON go back inside.) (To WINDSOR.)* Looks like we're more secure than you thought. Good night.

WINDSOR: You're not having an affair?

CACTUS: What are you talking about? No!

WINDSOR: Well, then, are you gonna be around? I'd like to see you.

CACTUS: No! We're closing up, going home. You should too, Cinderella.

WINDSOR: I turned into a pumpkin. After I was pricked by a Cactus. Buy you a drink?

CACTUS: I don't think so.

WINDSOR: Come on. You already ruined my plans.

CACTUS: Stuart, I'm sure you have things to do. You know, the Ball? The Mayor?

WINDSOR: The Mayor can wait. I'm gonna stay here till you say yes.

CACTUS: You'll freeze!

WINDSOR: That's all right. If I were a bum freezing in the street you'd like me better. I know. I'll let you save me. *(HE lurches to the fire escape.)* I'll just come on up.

CACTUS: You can't do that!

WINDSOR: Don't worry, I'll be easy to save. I won't struggle.

(WINDSOR begins to climb.)

CACTUS: You'll break your neck!
WINDSOR: Great! Even better than freezing.
CACTUS: I'm not kidding, you could get hurt.
WINDSOR: *(Grandly.)* What is danger, when love is indicted? I mean involved.
CACTUS: You'll ruin your tuxedo.
WINDSOR: I don't care. I own it!
CACTUS: Stuart, please stop that, and get down. I've got a few things to wrap up here. Then, why don't I meet you someplace later?
WINDSOR: *(Stops climbing.)* You're not kidding me now, are you?
CACTUS: I just don't know how long I'll be. Will you wait for me?
WINDSOR: You're always kidding me ...
CACTUS: I promise.
WINDSOR: Really? *(HE backs down the ladder.)* I could wait for you at Rivers. It's just like a party in there. Better than the Mayor's Ball.
CACTUS: Sounds great. Absolutely. I swear.
WINDSOR: *(HE squints up at her.)* There's something wrong with this picture.
CACTUS: Only because you're a little fuzzy ... *(WINDSOR waits for her to go inside. HE seems unsure what to do next.)* Great. Way to go, O'Riley. Good night.

(CACTUS goes through the window back into the office.)

FRED: Don't worry, with any luck, he'll pass out in the alley.
CACTUS: Why's Windsor hanging around here?
FRED: He has a crush on you. It's irritating, but it's not a

crime. Besides, he's drunk.

CACTUS: That's not like him. He's not the kind to change plans on a whim. We may think these guys need a second chance, but they're wanted. Stuart could really screw things up on this case.

FRED: "Case"? Did you say "case"? What does it matter if you're going to shut down the business?

CACTUS: Well, I have to get them out of here in order to close the office. So maybe that involves taking the case!

FRED: Quitter.

CACTUS: I am not a quitter!

ADELAIDE: You can't quit now, Cactus. We're just getting started.

(WINDSOR climbs up the fire escape, slams the window up and falls into the room, winding up flat on his back.)

WINDSOR: Cactus, what are you doing up there? God, you look pretty in the moonlight. Cactus. You were made for moonlight. Or is it just the neon light, or maybe ... Christmas lights? And that ... incendiary hair. Inflammatory mouth. Hot temper. Stop burning me, O'Riley!

CACTUS: Stuart Windsor?!

ADELAIDE: Fabulous! Another suspect!

End Act 1

ACT II

TIME

A few moments later.

PLACE

In the office.

AT CURTAIN

WINDSOR is dusting himself off. The others are staring at him. HE is still a bit off balance from his drinking.

· · · · ·

CACTUS: *(Furious.)* I said I'd meet you later.
WINDSOR: *(Singing to the tune of "Deck the Halls.")* "Pull the whiskers off of Santa, fa la la la la, la la la la ..."
CACTUS: What are you doing?
WINDSOR: I'm joining the party! I got cold just waiting for you. And a guy could wait forever. And, by the way, that window lock *is* faulty.
RAMON: Bring it up with the union. I did my job.
CACTUS: We're working in here. You could have knocked.

WINDSOR: On the window?
CACTUS: You could have used the door. *(SHE opens it.)* You can use it now.
WINDSOR: I already used the door. *(HE shuts it.)* It got me nowhere. Besides, you don't have a chimney. Ho, ho, ho.
CACTUS: Stuart, what's gotten into you?
WINDSOR: The Christmas Spirit! *(Looking around.)* Having a party?
ADELAIDE: Yes, we are!
WINDSOR: Hmm. *(Put out.)* Not invited, I guess. You didn't tell me it was a party here.
ADELAIDE: Of course you're invited.
CACTUS: No, Stuart, you're not. Please leave.
ADELAIDE: She said that to me, too. It's her way of getting you to stay.
WINDSOR: Why didn't I think of that? Cactus, please don't go to the Ball with me.
ADELAIDE: And who are you?
WINDSOR: I'm Stuart Windsor.

(WINDSOR extends his hand.)

ADELAIDE: I'm Adelaide Booker, Fred's mother. And what do you do, Mr. Windsor?
WINDSOR: Call me Stuart. I'm the ... *(Long pause.)* Deputy District Attorney. An old friend of Katie's, here.
ADELAIDE: Katie?
CACTUS: Cactus!
WINDSOR: We go back, way back ...

(RAMON and SMEDLEY hear that WINDSOR is the Deputy

DA. THEY turn their faces away and try to busy themselves behind the curtains, behind the couch, and try to edge their way to the door. FRED blocks their way.)

ADELAIDE: Well, the deputy District Attorney. And you're perfect for the role. You're probably incorruptible too.

CACTUS: Incoherent.

FRED: Inconvenient.

WINDSOR: I'm in-what? What role?

CACTUS: I'm sure you've got better things to do. The Christmas Ball?

WINDSOR: What's the Christmas Ball without a Christmas Cactus?

ADELAIDE: The role. It's the game, the murder mystery.

WINDSOR: Murder mystery? Game? I love games.

ADELAIDE: Everyone has a part. You're the crusading DA, he's the undercover cop. She's the detective. Right, Cactus?

CACTUS: Stuart, you won't enjoy this.

ADELAIDE: I'm the gun moll, and Fred ... Fred, what are you?

FRED: Speechless.

ADELAIDE: Ah yes. The silent partner. You see?

CACTUS: The parts are all taken.

WINDSOR: I've been playing games with Cactus for years. Most of her games are mysteries to me.

ADELAIDE: Fred, you never mentioned that this was a tradition!

WINDSOR: But I didn't get an invitation!

ADELAIDE: This is it!

CACTUS: About as much as I got for your stupid Ball!

WINDSOR: Spontaneity, my dear.

ADELAIDE: *(To WINDSOR.)* Believe me ...

CACTUS: Don't believe it.

ADELAIDE: This was all planned so carefully. No one knew. We were supposed to just stumble into it. That's part of the game.

WINDSOR: In that case, I wouldn't dream of missing it.

CACTUS: *(Changing tactics, SHE grabs the bottle and pours WINDSOR a drink.)* Well, then, here, Stuart, have a drink.

WINDSOR: What a good idea. A toast. But no one else is drinking. I don't drink alone. *(HE pours more drinks.)*

CACTUS: You just did.

WINDSOR: No, the bar was full. *(WINDSOR tries to get a good look at SMEDLEY and RAMON. HE pours them a drink.)* And our fellow merrymakers are ... ?

ADELAIDE: Actors. They've gone to so much trouble.

WINDSOR: Looks like a lot of trouble. *(WINDSOR inspects their outfits.)* Genuine city jail duds. *(To CACTUS.)* Did you swipe them? Or what?

FRED: They're rented.

CACTUS: *(Speaking at the same time as FRED.)* They're borrowed ... Stuart, maybe we should have a little chat here.

(CACTUS edges WINDSOR toward the door.)

WINDSOR: A chat?

CACTUS: The rules of the game, on my territory.

ADELAIDE: *(SHE gets out her notebook, looks it over and talks to WINDSOR with authority.)* This is Mr. Smedley, he's a convicted embezzler, but he's really very innocent. And Mr. Ramirez is an illegal alien. But for now they're both fugitives on the run. They're doing such a good job of it.

(SMEDLEY and RAMON cringe.)

SMEDLEY: It's a game.
RAMON: Un juego.
WINDSOR: *(Trying to put two and two together.)* Quite a job! Could it be that they escaped from a jail bus? ... What a coincidence!
FRED: We try for an authentic look.
WINDSOR: Really? Do you know that just today, the strangest thing ...

(CACTUS abruptly shuts WINDSOR up by kissing him. Then SHE grabs a Christmas cookie and shoves it in his mouth. A lively "Jingle Bells" comes up from the street.)

ADELAIDE: (Teasing SMEDLEY.) I guess you beat her to it, Mr. Kissing Bandit.
FRED: Unorthodox interrogation methods ...
SMEDLEY: If we'd only met under other circumstances.

(CACTUS pulls WINDSOR across the office, trying to find some private space. Meanwhile, ADELAIDE looks around, sees the plant, reads WINDSOR's note and finds the gun. ADELAIDE lifts it quietly and slips it into her purse. SMEDLEY watches her. SHE puts her finger to her lips to silence him.)

CACTUS: Will you listen to me?
WINDSOR: You're obstructing justice. But I'm a reasonable man. Do it again.

CACTUS: I'm really sorry about that.
WINDSOR: Don't apologize.
CACTUS: I realize that wasn't strictly professional.
WINDSOR: I'm sure you'll get better with practice.
CACTUS: Will you please trust me here?
WINDSOR: Trust you? Kiss me first. I'll trust you in a minute.
CACTUS: Hold on .... Fred, start looking through your desk. Look over very piece of paper. All that leftover stuff of Marley's. See if he had friends in high places.
FRED: I know what's in my desk!
CACTUS: Turn the drawers upside down.
ADELAIDE: If you protest, Fred, we'll suspect you. *(To CACTUS.)* You two pow-wow. We're examining the premises. Boys, over here. *(ADELAIDE motions the men to help her with the desk. THEY remove the papers and examine the contents, etc.)* Wait, let me get my list. Now, Mr. Marley's dead, so I'll just draw a little tombstone by his name.
CACTUS: Stuart ...
WINDSOR: *(Sobering up rapidly.)* You've never kissed me before. Not recently, anyway.
CACTUS: Don't start, Stuart.
WINDSOR: Something's going on here. I don't know what it is ...
CACTUS: A little game, a party. That's Fred's mother and I don't want you upsetting her ... Adelaide's been dropping hints about a murdery mystery party. So Fred and I set it up here tonight. It's her Christmas present.
WINDSOR: So this is how you operate, you confuse the issues.
CACTUS: Comes naturally. Want a drink?
WINDSOR: No.

CACTUS: This isn't your kind of party, Stuart.

WINDSOR: I don't know what this is really, but I think it's the kind of thing the DA would frown on. I can feel it ...

CACTUS: Don't be silly.

WINDSOR: I heard the police news today ...

CACTUS: Have a cookie.

(CACTUS grabs a cookie. WINDSOR stops her from feeding it to him.)

WINDSOR: I'd like to see you in a plea bargain situation.

CACTUS: Not a chance.

WINDSOR: I'm wondering, Katie, does the word "accessory" mean anything to you?

CACTUS: What about the words "justice" and "innocence"?

WINDSOR: Innocence? Where did you come up with that?

CACTUS: These two guys are as dangerous as marshmallow bullets.

WINDSOR: So they are who I think they are?

CACTUS: You'd never understand.

WINDSOR: Try me! Cactus, the boys in blue are out there thick tonight and they're not looking for reindeer!

CACTUS: I'm aware of that! But I could be looking at a big crack in the corruption at City Hall.

WINDSOR: Dream on, no one's been able to touch it.

ADELAIDE: I'm drawing a sawhorse next to Sawdust Construction.

CACTUS: You've got to let me work this my own way. *(CACTUS goes to the bookshelf and pulls a volume out, muttering to herself.)* Details. Details.

WINDSOR: What is it with you? Do you always have to be

the Lone Ranger? If you're in trouble, maybe I can help.

CACTUS: You can't. Stuart, do you want to send a poor, framed schnook back to jail?

WINDSOR: I'm not the enemy.

CACTUS: Stuart, sometimes you just ... gotta go with your guts. *(Reading the title.) The Old Curiosity Shop.*

(SHE tosses the volume carelessly. RAMON quickly steps forward to catch it. HE handles it gently and peruses it.)

WINDSOR: Satisfy my curiosity ...

ADELAIDE: Now Neville, what kind of symbol for the stolen money?

SMEDLEY: How about a dollar bill with wings?

ADELAIDE: Of course.

CACTUS: Let me have a little time. I'm asking you as a friend. Give me tonight.

WINDSOR: For what?

CACTUS: I have to find something that will prove Smedley didn't embezzle the Children's Hospital fund. *(SHE looks through another volume, shaking out the pages, and talking to herself.)* They're just leather-bound books.

RAMON: You must be careful with that!

WINDSOR: The "Tiny Tim fund"? That embezzlement?

FRED: Don't forget Chuck.

CACTUS: Shh. Be quiet ...

ADELAIDE: No fair, if you've got something, you have to share it.

CACTUS: And if it isn't here, it probably doesn't exist.

WINDSOR: Smedley ... Smedley ... I remember.

ADELAIDE: Time's up.

A CHRISTMAS CACTUS

CACTUS: *(Thinking aloud.)* Marley was probably the kind of loon for minutia who thinks secret codes are a good time. *(To WINDSOR.)* Please. Just leave and pretend you weren't here.

WINDSOR: And if I don't?

CACTUS: Give me a break, Stuart.

WINDSOR: I'm not leaving.

CACTUS: Stuart ...

WINDSOR: No. I'm playing your game. I want to watch you operate. Maybe I'll get kissed again. Maybe I'll have you arrested.

CACTUS: Don't count on it. What do you think you're going to do, be the good guy?

WINDSOR: You don't like good guys. *(THEY go back to the others at the desk. ADELAIDE wanders near the bookcase. WINDSOR whispers to CACTUS.)* I am not leaving you alone here. And I'll give you time. God, I must be drunk. But don't try and shake me this time.

ADELAIDE: It's just full of novels. This is a detective's office. But look at this, no Chandler, no Hammett, and where's Agatha Christie? *(SHE shakes her head.)* Dickens!

CACTUS: The Dickens are mine, Adelaide. *(Distracted by another book, CACTUS looks for something but doesn't find it. SHE moves to the lamp and puts the book under it.)* Nothing!

WINDSOR: What are you talking about?

CACTUS: Nothing's underlined or marked. No pages turned.

RAMON: These books should be handled gently, with respect. See how beautiful they are.

(CACTUS opens the pages and holds them up to the light, examining them. RAMON stands by nervously.)

FRED: What are you doing?

CACTUS: There could be impressions made by a pen. Letters marked to devise a message. Invisible ink.

WINDSOR: *(Sarcastic.)* Invisible ink! Why didn't I think of that? You don't get too many invisible ink cases these days.

CACTUS: Watch it, wise guy.

(SHE tosses the book. RAMON goes in for the second save.)

SMEDLEY: *(Edging toward the door.)* Ramon, maybe we should say goodbye.

WINDSOR: The game's not over yet, gentlemen.

(THEY freeze.)

CACTUS: *(To SMEDLEY and RAMON.)* Wait. He's going to give us some time.

SMEDLEY: It's all over. We're never going to find it. It's back to the cellblock.

RAMON: But you are not there now.

SMEDLEY: One day, one lousy day. Is that all I'm gonna get?

CACTUS: Take it while you can. What have you found?

ADELAIDE: We've gone over just about everything in the desk. Who knows?

FRED: *(HE's going through boxes.)* Nothing of Marley's, except some old office supplies. Tape, folders, forms.

SMEDLEY: *(HE is struck by something.)* Wait a minute, that looks familiar. It's a city purchase order, and it's blank.

WINDSOR: What's that doing here?

CACTUS: *(SHE compares it with one in SMEDLEY'S file.)*

They're the same. Fred, how many of these are there?

FRED: Small box, about 200.

CACTUS: *(SHE pulls a tab from the bottom of the box.)* The packing slip. It's addressed to Marley.

FRED: He must have ordered them.

SMEDLEY: *(Picking up a pen from the desk, HE writes on the page.)* Look, the signature goes all the way through, but on the top line, the payee ... nothing. They could have changed the name. *(HE suddenly realizes.)* That's *how* they did it. The part I didn't figure out. All the checks were cashed. None of the names on the checks existed, but my name was all over the order.

ADELAIDE: What does it mean?

WINDSOR: Don't look at me. I'm just an accessory. She's the sleuth.

CACTUS: It means Marley knew. He was in on the fraud.

SMEDLEY: That's right. He knew! He had to know!

CACTUS: It doesn't clear you. It just means Marley was involved. He was a crook. What was the motive? *(SHE shakes her head.)* Everybody's got a motive. *(CACTUS pulls out another novel and another. RAMON gets ready to catch them.)* There's got to be something here. Besides Victorian excess.

WINDSOR: *The Life and Adventures of Martin Chuzzlewit.*

(This time WINDSOR tosses the book and RAMON saves it.)

RAMON: Not his best. But still you should take care with it.

ADELAIDE: Cactus. It's time to put our cards on the table.

SMEDLEY: What, Adelaide?

ADELAIDE: Motives. Mr. Marley is dead. Who had the strongest desire to "remove" him?

WINDSOR: Marley? Jake Marley? But he's dead.

ADELAIDE: A little slow on the uptake.

CACTUS: You knew Marley?

WINDSOR: Yeah.

CACTUS: What was he like, what did you think of him?

WINDSOR: He was just a mousy little guy.

CACTUS: How'd you know him?

WINDSOR: He helped us on four or five big cases. Embezzlement, mostly. He was sort of a genius at spotting faked accounts. Kind of a specialty of his.

CACTUS: Maybe he could spot 'em because he designed them.

ADELAIDE: I know, Mr. Windsor. He knew you faked your expense account, so you wouldn't mind seeing Marley dead.

WINDSOR: Not guilty! I hardly knew him.

CACTUS: You also knew Neville Smedley.

WINDSOR: Not personally. But I remember the DA's case on him.

CACTUS: Holding back your aces, huh?

RAMON: But what are you looking for in the books?

CACTUS: I'm not sure.

FRED: I love it when she free associates. Something just clicks.

RAMON: Clicks?

FRED: It clicks. And she wants to give it all up.

RAMON: Give what up?

FRED: The office. The job. The mission. She wants to close us down.

RAMON: I don't believe it.

CACTUS: Stuart, if we find something, something indicating he was framed, I want you to cut a deal for Smedley to go free on bond, pending a new trial.

(CACTUS continues to pull books out of the case. RAMON tries to hold all the books in his arms.)

WINDSOR: *(Reading over CACTUS's shoulder.)* Hmmm. *Great Expectations?* That's a pretty big order, lady. I don't know about a deal, the guy's an escaped convict.

CACTUS: Don't give me that, Stuart Windsor. You are the king of "Let's Make a Deal" down there.

WINDSOR: You don't like deals ...

CACTUS: Not when they're guilty! But this guy ...

SMEDLEY: No one ever offered me a deal.

WINDSOR: You don't get a deal if you don't cop a plea.

SMEDLEY: I didn't do it!

CACTUS: Look at him, Stuart. Do you honestly think he was capable of embezzling all that money?

WINDSOR: Well, as I recall, no one could really figure out how the doofus did it so clean. But the evidence was overwhelming. The cancelled bank checks, files tampered with, dual accounts. Everything checked out. It all had Smedley's name on it. He was with the city. He had *access*. Means. Opportunity.

SMEDLEY: I wouldn't steal money from those kids.

WINDSOR: *(Tiredly.)* Everyone says they're innocent.

CACTUS: And Marley supplied all the evidence?

WINDSOR: That's right.

CACTUS: *(SHE takes a purchase order for emphasis.)* And he did it with this. He was in on the frame. Recover any of the money?

WINDSOR: No, as a matter of fact.

(HE looks at SMEDLEY.)

SMEDLEY: Well, I don't have it! If I had it I wouldn't be here.

CACTUS: Doesn't that suggest something to you?

WINDSOR: If it was Marley who framed Smedley - then who was he working for?

CACTUS: Scum always floats to the top.

FRED: That would be the Mayor.

ADELAIDE: The Mayor! You didn't say anything about the Mayor! *(ADELAIDE refers to her list.)* I'm putting the Mayor at the top of the list, so he gets a little gavel.

WINDSOR: That could explain why we never found the money. *(CACTUS nods.)* Nice theory, but Marley's dead. And you have no evidence.

CACTUS: *(SHE gets another book to examine.)* Not yet! *A Tale of Two Cities.*

RAMON: Please, Cactus. More gently.

ADELAIDE: I can't wait to question the Mayor! *(SHE checks her list.)* I know one thing, though. Fred couldn't do it.

FRED: Don't be silly, Adelaide, of course I could do it. I wanted Marley dead, because ... because he was scum. Everyone knew that.

ADELAIDE: Lots of people are scum, Fred.

FRED: He was ... creme de la scum.

ADELAIDE: You'll have to do better than that, Frederick.

FRED: My own mother doesn't think I'm capable of murder. Well, Adelaide, just maybe I am. You want a motive, I'll give you a motive. I wanted this office. The rents in this town are ridiculous. Everyone knows that. I wanted Marley out of the way so Cactus and I could open our business and solve crimes. So there.

CACTUS: Fred, I am impressed.

ADELAIDE: Oh Frederick. No one would kill for an office lease. That's silly.

FRED: But Adelaide, this building is rent-controlled.

ADELAIDE: Really! *(Impressed.)* Oh, well, that's different. That's my boy! *(ADELAIDE casts her eye on RAMON.)* And you, Mr. Ramirez ...

RAMON: I wanted to find him alive! Believe me. I respect his taste in literature too much. Besides, books teach us that murder is not a good idea. It always fires back.

(HE holds out a book for emphasis.)

CACTUS: Backfires, Ramon.

ADELAIDE: *(Delighted.)* A likely story. Maybe you killed him for this collection! Even if it *is* Dickens.

SMEDLEY: Oh, what's the use! I'm going back, we won't find anything to clear me. I wanted to kill him. I came here tonight to kill him.

RAMON: You are not helping yourself, amigo.

SMEDLEY: I was gonna make him admit he knew the evidence was phony. I was gonna make him give me a green card for Ramon here. Then I was gonna kill Marley. Like he deserved. Only when I got here, Red, here, Detective O'Riley, told me he was already dead.

ADELAIDE: *(Brightly.)* We're cooking now! What's your motive, Cactus?

CACTUS: My motive? *(Irritated.)* I am the investigator in

this case! I am not a suspect. I am the private eye, the gumshoe, the dick, the flatfoot, the sleuth and the shamus. In other words, I am the detective. Being a detective is not your everyday 9-to-5 working stiff kind of a job. It takes certain talents. Talents that I have. Is that clear?

ADELAIDE: Well, if you're going to be a stickler for the rules ...

WINDSOR: Nah, Cactus is making up her own rules again. She's always doing that.

CACTUS: Somewhere along the line Marley sold out for dirty money. He turned his back on the profession.

ADELAIDE: Then, of course, there's *my* motive.

FRED: Your motive?

ADELAIDE: Yes. Neville was in the slammer at the time of Mr. Marley's demise, but I, as Neville's faithful gun moll, would have wanted revenge on the treacherous Marley. And who would have suspected me?

FRED: I certainly wouldn't.

ADELAIDE: Don't get snippy, Fred, I could do it.

RAMON: Why would a nice lady like you kill the bad man?

ADELAIDE: For the most compelling reason. Passion.

(ADELAIDE moves toward SMEDLEY.)

WINDSOR: *(Looking at CACTUS.)* I see. Of course. I believe in passion.

ADELAIDE: *(Seriously.)* But there's a problem, as I see it. Neville really had the strongest motive, but he lacked the opportunity. Everyone else had the opportunity, but not a strong enough motive. Anyway, that leaves me, but it couldn't be me. At least I don't think I killed him. No one has told me

I killed him. I'd think I should know. Oh, it's obvious! The game's not over yet. We have to find more clues.

CACTUS: I need to find out more about Marley. Did he ever buy into the romance of it? What was he like when he started out?

WINDSOR: Precious little romance here.

CACTUS: Why don't you go through that old file cabinet.

(WINDSOR does. CACTUS goes to the bookcase and reaches out for another volume.)

WINDSOR: This doesn't look like a file. *(HE takes out a Christmas box and withdraws a pretty silk nightgown.)* Wow. *(Looks at CACTUS.)* This is murder.

ADELAIDE: So another woman is involved in the crime.

CACTUS: *(SHE runs over and grabs the nightgown.)* Give me that!

WINDSOR: You told me to look in there. I didn't know it was the L-for-Lingerie file.

CACTUS: I forgot that was in there.

WINDSOR: Who is it for? Your sainted mother?

CACTUS: No, wise guy. It's a present from my Aunt Maureen, to cheer me up at Christmas.

WINDSOR: It's certainly cheering me up.

CACTUS: Is that a crime?

ADELAIDE: *(Suspiciously.)* That's not the kind of gift an aunt would give.

RAMON: It is a fine gift.

FRED: Somebody must have spent a fortune.

CACTUS: *(SHE nods.)* Christian Dior. *(CACTUS folds it up and puts it back.)* It'll probably just go in a drawer.

WINDSOR: That would be a shame.

ADELAIDE: Look, there's another present under the tree. Another clue.

(CACTUS moans.)

SMEDLEY: You don't get presents in jail.
ADELAIDE: Not even from your gun moll?
RAMON: Perhaps we will find what you're looking for.
SMEDLEY: Not for me. Not for Smedley.
ADELAIDE: Oh, Neville.
CACTUS: *(SHE takes out a wrapped box and tosses it to SMEDLEY.)* Here, catch, and stop whining.
SMEDLEY: For me? *(Ripping it open.)* Candy! Chocolates. All different kinds! I love chocolate. *(HE takes a piece of it, stuffing one in his mouth. HE offers the box to ADELAIDE.)* Have one.
ADELAIDE: Well, it certainly looks delicious.

(SHE glances at CACTUS and FRED.)

CACTUS AND FRED: It's not poisoned!
ADELAIDE: In that case ...

(ADELAIDE takes one and offers them out.)

CACTUS: Okay, paint me a picture of Marley. Anyone ...
SMEDLEY: He was a framing, conniving snake!
CACTUS: Suppose that Jake had a secret life. He certainly was privy to secrets. Worked on city contracts. He liked working with numbers.

ADELAIDE: He had a woman that no one knew about. She was dangerous.

RAMON: He loved beautiful books.

(RAMON stands guard by the books.)

FRED: He had a sweet tooth.

CACTUS: What did he leave behind?

FRED: A box of phony city purchase orders.

WINDSOR: The money was never recovered on the Tiny Tim scam.

CACTUS: The only personal indications are that he had an odd affection for Dickens. Hmm. Jake Marley. Dickens. What are we missing here?

WINDSOR: So, nothing valuable. No estate. No family.

CACTUS: He was the middle man. He had information.

ADELAIDE: And it was valuable enough for someone to kill him for it.

CACTUS: Or killed him just to keep him quiet.

WINDSOR: So what was the weapon of choice? Knife? Gun?

CACTUS: *(To herself.)* The gun? Oh my God! *(CACTUS goes to the plant, looking for the gun. It's not there, so SHE starts hunting frantically on the desk, under the plant, on the floor, opening the drawers.) (To SMEDLEY.)* Where is it?

SMEDLEY: I don't have it. Honestly.

WINDSOR: What's going on?

CACTUS: *(To WINDSOR.)* Nothing. *(To SMEDLEY.)* Well?

FRED: Just the game, Stuart. You know, a red herring to throw us off balance.

WINDSOR: More like a redhead throwing us off balance.

ADELAIDE: *(With a sly grin.)* Are you looking for

something?
   CACTUS: Yes, I am.
   ADELAIDE: Was it something you *planted?*
   CACTUS: Maybe it was.
   ADELAIDE: Maybe I know something. Maybe I found a clue.
   CACTUS: Maybe you should give it to the nice detective.
   WINDSOR: Maybe you should give it to the nice DA.
   ADELAIDE: *(Pleased.)* But I'm the gun moll. Who better to have a gun?

(ADELAIDE pulls the gun triumphantly out of her purse.)

   CACTUS: Give me that.
   WINDSOR: Adelaide, be careful. That could have prints.
   ADELAIDE: Of course. You're right.

(ADELAIDE pulls a handkerchief from her purse and wipes the gun thoroughly.)

   WINDSOR: No. Don't do that!

(ADELAIDE blithely eludes WINDSOR.)

   RAMON: Please, Señora, you would not want to hurt anyone.
   ADELAIDE: It was filthy. When I pulled it out of the plant, it had dirt all over its snout.
   WINDSOR: The Christmas Cactus? How'd it get there?
   CACTUS: Beats me. You brought it, Stuart.
   WINDSOR: Wait a minute.
   RAMON: *(To WINDSOR.) You* put the gun in the plant?
   ADELAIDE: *(Excited.)* Maybe I was meant to find it. Maybe

I *am* the murderer. *(SHE spins around, gun held high, and trips over FRED's suitcase. EVERYONE ducks.)* Why, it's a suitcase. How did it get here?

SMEDLEY: Looks like someone's leaving town.

ADELAIDE: *(FRED helps her up.)* The murderer, of course. Whoever it belongs to is the murderer.

(FRED picks it up. CACTUS takes the gun gently from ADELAIDE.)

CACTUS: It's not you, Adelaide. You're much too ... nice.

FRED: *(Wildly.)* It's me! I did it. I'm your man!

RAMON: You did it? I never suspected you.

FRED: Yes, of course, you fools. See, here are my initials. FMB - Fred "Mad Dog" Booker. I planned it from the start. And it was easy. He had money, he stashed it away. Buckets of it. Marley walked right into my trap. Harmless old Fred. Everyone was suckered. Now I've the clues, and the cash. And I'm leaving for the warm waters of the Caribbean. Now I have to run. Furthermore, I've got my ticket. To Martinique. I'm leaving the day after tomorrow. And no one's stopping me. Do you hear me! No one!

ADELAIDE: Bravo, Fred! *(SHE claps.)*

WINDSOR: You did it? What about the gun?

CACTUS: *(SHE locks it up in her file cabinet.)* A toy gun. A prop.

WINDSOR: I'd like to see it.

CACTUS: You saw it.

WINDSOR: I could insist.

(SMEDLEY sits down, depressed.)

ADELAIDE: *(Delighted with herself.)* Why so glum, Neville? We solved the mystery. The murderer is my son, Fred. Now let's have a drink.

FRED: Adelaide, before this goes any further, I have to tell you something.

ADELAIDE: I know, darling. You were brilliant.

SMEDLEY: It's not going to work. We didn't find anything to clear me.

RAMON: If you give in to despair, my friend, I will lose my faith in the miracle.

SMEDLEY: Miracle!

RAMON: It has to be a miracle. Tonight Teresa will pray for me as I have been praying.

SMEDLEY: Well, it doesn't work. It's a big fat nothing.

ADELAIDE: Don't worry, there's a solution. You can't write a mystery without a solution at the end.

CACTUS: Something still bothers me about the books. They don't fit with the office. (*CACTUS hands everyone a book.*) *Nicholas Nickelby, Oliver Twist, David Copperfield.* Open them up. Shake them out. You too, Ramon. Don't sneer, Stuart. We're looking for anything. Slips of paper ... See if something catches your eye. Is there anything underlined? Highlighted? Are page corners turned?

WINDSOR: Book abuser.

FRED: Adelaide, we have to talk ...

ADELAIDE: Not now, Fred.

FRED: I'm going to Martinique for Christmas, Adelaide.

ADELAIDE: Of course you are. You're a fugitive from justice.

FRED: I am!

ADELAIDE: I know.

FRED: I give up.

SMEDLEY: *(HE buries his head in his hands.)* Oh God. It's just like he's here.

FRED: Who's here, Smedley?

SMEDLEY: Marley, Marley's ghost. Laughing at us. Getting the last laugh.

CACTUS: Wait a minute. Chuck! *(The others turn to look at her. ADELAIDE comforts SMEDLEY. CACTUS takes the hat off the bust of Dickens and stares at it.)* ... If it's really Charles Dickens.

FRED: Yes, yes, it's definitely Chuck. Look at the beard.

RAMON: We already decided that.

ADELAIDE: Charles Dickens. But he's dead too. Does anyone know how he died?

SMEDLEY: Who knows what he looked like?

FRED: *(FRED grabs the bust.)* He looked like this!

CACTUS: No! Think! This office was ransacked last week.

FRED: But nothing was taken.

CACTUS: Because there wasn't anything valuable. Chuck wasn't here.

FRED: He was doing time at the local elementary school library.

CACTUS: *(Thinking aloud.)* And last year, the burglars may not have known what to look for so they had to go all the way back around Marley's life, turned up empty-handed, and came back.

FRED: That's preposterous.

(CACTUS starts tapping on the bust, then thumping on it and listening.)

WINDSOR: You can't tell me this thing is valuable.

CACTUS: This sucker is hollow. *(CACTUS picks up the bust, shakes it, and turns it over.)* Fred, give me that letter opener, will you? *(FRED hands it over. CACTUS fiddles with the bottom of the bust. SHE turns it upside down and out fall some documents and a key.)* Bank books. "Jacob Marley." And a key. Looks like it belongs to a safety deposit box.

FRED: *(Opening one of the bank books.)* This guy was loaded!

CACTUS: Quite a private stash.

SMEDLEY: He hoarded it?

WINDSOR: The middle man?

CACTUS: He didn't make this kind of money doing the straight stuff.

SMEDLEY: *(Picking up a bank book.)* We could match these deposit dates to the payouts of city checks.

WINDSOR: This doesn't prove anything except that he didn't live to enjoy it.

RAMON: *(His arms are full of books.)* I was wondering ... I don't see the Scrooge book. Did you read that one?

CACTUS: *A Christmas Carol?*

WINDSOR: Didn't everyone?

CACTUS: It's not here. How many books did Dickens write?

RAMON: More than 30. Depending on which anthology you use as to the exact number.

(FRED goes over to his suitcase, opens it up and brings the book to CACTUS.)

FRED: You got me. More evidence. I'm going to read it in Martinique ...

CACTUS: *(SHE leafs through it.)* This isn't *A Christmas Carol!*

WINDSOR: What are you talking about?

CACTUS: It looks like it must have been his day book, or a log of some kind. Inside. Look. It's a false cover over a few pages of the novel. The inside is full of handwriting.

WINDSOR: Let me see.

(CACTUS and WINDSOR tussle over the book.)

CACTUS: Don't grab.

WINDSOR: Stand still.

CACTUS: Don't read over my shoulder. I hate that.

WINDSOR: How am I supposed to read it? What are those numbers?

CACTUS: Fred, come here, please. These numbers ... here in the beginning.

FRED: They look like file numbers.

ADELAIDE: *(Joining them.)* What's going on?

SMEDLEY: That's what I'd like to know.

CACTUS: Yes, but it looks like they correspond to another set of numbers.

SMEDLEY: You got something? You finally got something?

CACTUS: This must be his own code.

ADELAIDE: I'm sure you're getting somewhere, but didn't we already solve it?

(A little confused, ADELAIDE gets her list out and goes over it.)

RAMON: Where are we getting? The Mass will begin.

Teresa will be joining the procession.

CACTUS: Fred, the file. Get me Smedley's file.

(FRED hands CACTUS the file. SHE looks at the number on it and checks it against the log. CACTUS and WINDSOR briefly struggle over the book again in their excitement.)

CACTUS: It's my office!

WINDSOR: Okay, okay.

CACTUS: *(Going over the book.)* The guy was obsessed with details. Smedley, this is the ...

WINDSOR: *(Cutting in.)* The case on the Tiny Tim Fund!

CACTUS: How it really happened. Looks like everything's here. Even a description of how he planned the case against you.

SMEDLEY: I knew it, I knew it! But why me?

CACTUS: "F. for Fezziwig." Suited his sense of humor and it fit the pattern. He refers you as Fezziwig. Dickens. Marley. Fezziwig!

SMEDLEY: I always hated that name.

ADELAIDE: What kind of criminal keeps records of how he committed his crime?

FRED: Blackmailers keep great files.

CACTUS: *(Thinking out loud.)* Say somebody in the city government embezzles an account. Then he hires Marley to frame a fall guy for it. Marley blackmails whoever hires him ... He'd keep records of everything.

WINDSOR: Well, his specialty was faked accounts.

CACTUS: He's even noted his fee from the city for the investigation, with the check number written down. There must be 20 chapter headings here. Twenty cases. "Sawdust

A CHRISTMAS CACTUS 81

Construction." Don't you see, Stuart, Smedley's not the only one who's been framed. Those files and this book ... think of the implications.

WINDSOR: Well, you'll just have to turn them all over to me.
CACTUS: Not so fast. You know the procedure, Counselor.
WINDSOR: But you have all the groundwork.
CACTUS: And you have nothing without me.
WINDSOR: You want to deal, don't you?
CACTUS: I'm sure we can work something out. What about Smedley?
SMEDLEY: This clears me! Adelaide!
ADELAIDE: That's wonderful.
WINDSOR: If only he'd gone through regular channels.
CACTUS: There were no regular channels to go through!
SMEDLEY: But I'm innocent! This proves it!
WINDSOR: There'll be some jail time.
SMEDLEY: *(Horrified.)* Go back?
ADELAIDE: Wait a minute, if we've solved it, then why are you ... still ... so excited?

(ADELAIDE thinks about it. SHE takes the file on SMEDLEY and looks it over again.)

WINDSOR: It would look good if you turned yourself in. Look chum, we've got time to straighten this all out.
CACTUS: Stuart, you could find a judge, set bond, show the evidence, call a press conference. You'll be a hero.
ADELAIDE: *(SHE picks up a yellowed news clipping from the case.)* This looks real.
CACTUS: There'll be a reward. Of course *you* don't qualify, but the rest of us would, if it leads to recovery of city funds ...

ADELAIDE: It is real, isn't it? Oh my, oh my.

(ADELAIDE sits down shakily.)

SMEDLEY: Adelaide. I ... I ... uh. It's true. We kept telling you the truth.

(SMEDLEY approaches ADELAIDE. SHE sidles away from him suspiciously.)

CACTUS: Good enough for you, Counselor?
WINDSOR: Where am I supposed to find a judge on Christmas Eve?
CACTUS: The bars are still open. And you're a member of the Bar ...
WINDSOR: Maybe we could use the press on this one. Public opinion could give us some leverage.
CACTUS: I knew you'd find the right angle.
WINDSOR: Surprised?
CACTUS: Actually, yes.

(CACTUS and WINDSOR face each other, and slowly move together. ADELAIDE stands up and breaks them apart.)

ADELAIDE: This charade was no charade, was it? I want the truth now!

(SHE looks at each person.)

FRED: Adelaide, listen ...
ADELAIDE: Frederick! This news clipping is real! Isn't it?

This wasn't a game. *(Her voice rises.)* Mr. Ramirez *is* an illegal alien, and Mr. Smedley *is* a convict. And you're both fugitives! *(Again, ADELAIDE sinks to the sofa. The others gather around her uneasily.)* It's real. Real. Real.

CACTUS: That's right, Adelaide. Tonight, instead of being here, you could have rearranged the tinsel on Fred's tree! You could have been safe and secure. Of course you never would have met Stuart or Ramon or Smedley here, who by the way, is innocent. You never would have played the game.

ADELAIDE: It wasn't a game!

CACTUS: Life is a game, Adelaide. Only this time, when we put the puzzle together, we won more than the plastic ring in the Crackerjacks box. We're going to redeem Smedley's fate. This round the good guys are going to win. How often do you hit the bullseye? Use your noggin, Adelaide. You were looking for excitement tonight. You were hungry for it. You were craving it. And you found it in the most unlikely place.

ADELAIDE: Then, it actually does mean that Neville is innocent?

WINDSOR: Looks that way.

SMEDLEY: Adelaide?

ADELAIDE: Neville? *(Getting excited.)* This is ... well ... it's, it's wonderful!

(THEY all look alarmed.)

FRED: Mother, are you all right?

ADELAIDE: Yes, dear. This wasn't just a murder mystery party. It was a real adventure. And you tried to fool me. Oh, wait till I tell my friends ... and Julia! This will make her parties look like amateur hour. Poisoned hors d'oeuvres. Ha!

SMEDLEY: You're not mad at me, Addie?

ADELAIDE: I just walked into it. All these years of reading books and hoping that maybe ... someday. Something happened to Adelaide Booker! Why ... it's thrilling! That's what it is! Thrilling!

CACTUS: Better than egg nog.

ADELAIDE: And, Mr. Windsor ... I expect you to have Neville out in time for Christmas dinner.

WINDSOR: I don't work miracles.

RAMON: No, but Someone does.

WINDSOR: There is a problem. A *gun* was reported missing from that pawnshop that the bus slammed into ...

CACTUS: You know how these things get misplaced.

WINDSOR: People don't misplace guns.

CACTUS: Oh, Stuart, stop worrying. You know they don't keep loaded guns in store windows anyway. It's illegal.

SMEDLEY: *(Stunned.)* They don't? You mean ...

CACTUS: *(To WINDSOR.)* It'll probably turn up in a few days at the pawnshop. Or in the mail.

WINDSOR: In the mail?

SMEDLEY: You're not half bad, for a lawyer. *(To RAMON.)* I'm going back with him, Ramon. I got a chance it'll work out for me. But I don't know about you. There isn't anything for you here.

WINDSOR: Ramon, you seem like a real decent fellow.

CACTUS: So what are you going to do?

RAMON: *(RAMON goes to the window and looks out.)* Teresa must be close now.

WINDSOR: Ramon, get out of here.

RAMON: I can go?

CACTUS: Don't ask twice.

WINDSOR: Look, I've got enough paperwork with this guy. If anyone asks, I never saw you.
RAMON: This is what I've been waiting for. *(To SMEDLEY.)* And you doubted a miracle.

(SMEDLEY shrugs and reaches out his hand to shake. RAMON bypasses the hand and hugs SMEDLEY.)

WINDSOR: You know you could be picked up at any time. They'll be out looking.

(Strains of "O Come, All Ye Faithful" are heard from the street.)

FRED: *(Taking off his jacket and handing it to RAMON.)* You can't very well go out like that.
CACTUS: Feliz Navidad. *(CACTUS grabs the boxed nightgown and hands it to RAMON.)* Here. Give this to Teresa. She'll love it.
RAMON: Gracias. Our first child, we will name it Cactus.

(RAMON exits out the window.)

CACTUS: Yeah, after the saint ... *(CACTUS watches him go. Then SHE looks at the others.)* It's late. Looks like the party's over ...

(CACTUS hands ADELAIDE her coat.)

ADELAIDE: *(SHE gets her things together.)* Why don't we all walk out together?

WINDSOR: *(To SMEDLEY.)* You want to come down and make a statement?
CACTUS: I'll bring Marley's log with me. For emphasis.
ADELAIDE: This was a wonderful present, Fred. Julia will be green with envy!
FRED: But it wasn't really a ... present.
ADELAIDE: Of course it was. The best ever ...
FRED: Adelaide, I have to tell you something about our vacation ...

(ADELAIDE's attention wanders.)

ADELAIDE: I'm going to be so busy ...
FRED: It's no use.
ADELAIDE: *(To SMEDLEY.)* You didn't say you'd come ... to Christmas dinner.
SMEDLEY: Of course, I'm coming, Addie.
ADELAIDE: Isn't that nice ...

(ADELAIDE pats SMEDLEY's face and HE holds her hand there.)

FRED: About the lease renewal?

(HE hands it to CACTUS with a pen. SHE signs it. SHE grimaces at him.)

CACTUS: Okay, one more year. I'll deliver it in person. Send me a postcard, will you?
FRED: Merry Christmas, Boss.

(HE kisses CACTUS.)

Cactus: Fred!
Fred: Mistletoe!
Cactus: *(Looking up.)* There's no ... mistletoe

(FRED grabs his suitcase and looks at ADELAIDE, who has eyes only for SMEDLEY. FRED exits in front of ADELAIDE, who doesn't even see him. FRED gives a jubilant wave to CACTUS.)

Windsor: Didn't I warn you about that guy? *(To the others.)* Do you mind waiting outside? We'll be down in a few minutes.
Smedley: Aren't you going to tell me not to leave town?
Windsor: Get out of here.

(ADELAIDE and SMEDLEY exit through the door. From the street below come the sounds of SINGING in the procession of Las Posadas. Candlelights reflect from outside.)

Cactus: You really came through for all of us, Stuart. For me ...
Windsor: Maybe I'm just that way around you.
Cactus: No, couldn't be me. I've never been very nice to you.
Windsor: You could start now.

(CACTUS looks out the window.)

CACTUS: Do you think he'll find Teresa out there?
WINDSOR: Why not? It's Christmas.
CACTUS: *(Softly.)* Maybe I could be nicer. A little.
WINDSOR: Maybe we could swing by that Ball.
CACTUS: The Ball!
WINDSOR: And hunt up a drunken judge or two. For Smedley.
CACTUS: Oh, okay. A drunken judge. Good idea.

(SHE gets her coat and heads for the door.)

WINDSOR: Not that way, O'Riley! This way. The way I came in.

(HE points to the window.)

CACTUS: You are a rake at heart, Stuart.
WINDSOR: Merry Christmas.
CACTUS: *(SHE follows him to the window.)* Happy New Year. Oh Stuart ...
WINDSOR: Yes?
CACTUS: Mistletoe.

(SHE quickly kisses him.)

Windsor: *(Grins.)* Mistletoe!

(THEY kiss and climb out the window to the fire escape. The CAROLING is stronger. The lights from the candle procession below flicker through the window. The SAXOPHONE joins in on a jubilant "Joy to the World.")

CURTAIN

COSTUME PLOT

CACTUS:
Stylish jacket, sweater or blouse, skirt, hat, coat & purse.

FRED: *Slacks, shirt, colorful sweater & jacket.*

WINDSOR: *Tuxedo, shirt, cummerbund & tie.*

SMEDLEY:
Jeans, blue workshirt with lettering, eg., COUNTY JAIL.

RAMON: *Same as SMEDLEY.*

ADELAIDE:
Good dress, suitable for a party; lace collar, pearls, coat, purse & handkerchief.

PROPS

Speaker phone
Suitcase with men's beach and swimwear, goggles, snorkel &
    suntan lotion
Vacation brochures
Bust of Charles Dickens with false bottom
Bank books, keys
Set of Charles Dickens novels
Box of Christmas ornaments
Plate of Christmas cookies
Christmas cards
Mail
Office supplies, pens, papers, clipboards, etc.
Notebooks
Darts for dartboard
Large Christmas Cactus plant
Small tape recorder
Bottle of liquor, six glasses
Several boxes of files with papers, newspaper clippings
Two revolvers
Nightgown in gift box
Gift box of candy

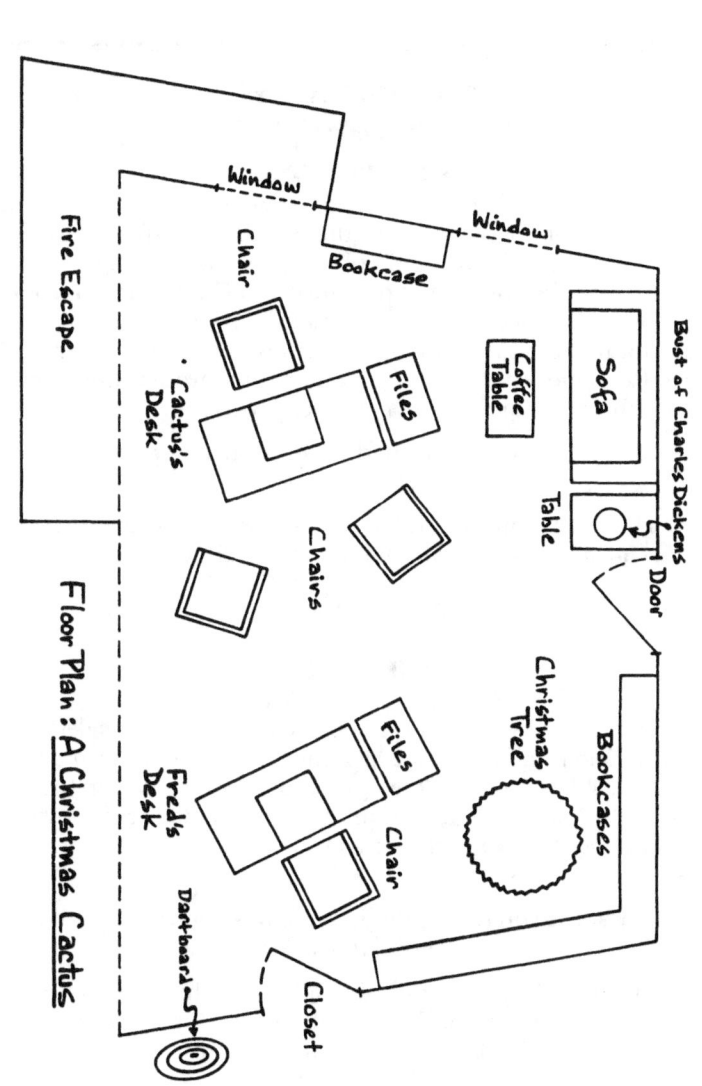

THE OFFICE PLAYS
Two full length plays by Adam Bock

THE RECEPTIONIST
Comedy / 2m., 2f. Interior

At the start of a typical day in the Northeast Office, Beverly deals effortlessly with ringing phones and her colleague's romantic troubles. But the appearance of a charming rep from the Central Office disrupts the friendly routine. And as the true nature of the company's business becomes apparent, The Receptionist raises disquieting, provocative questions about the consequences of complicity with evil.

"...Mr. Bock's poisoned Post-it note of a play."
- *New York Times*

"Bock's intense initial focus on the routine goes to the heart of *The Receptionist's* pointed, painfully timely allegory... elliptical, provocative play..."
- *Time Out New York*

THE THUGS
Comedy / 2m, 6f / Interior

The Obie Award winning dark comedy about work, thunder and the mysterious things that are happening on the 9th floor of a big law firm. When a group of temps try to discover the secrets that lurk in the hidden crevices of their workplace, they realize they would rather believe in gossip and rumors than face dangerous realities.

"Bock starts you off giggling, but leaves you with a chill."
- *Time Out New York*

"... a delightfully paranoid little nightmare that is both more chillingly realistic and pointedly absurd than anything John Grisham ever dreamed up."
- *New York Times*

SAMUELFRENCH.COM

www.ingramcontent.com/pod-product-compliance
Lightning Source LLC
Chambersburg PA
CBHW070646300426
44111CB00013B/2286